Greetings from Belleville
New Jersey

Anthony Buccino

GREETINGS FROM BELLEVILLE, NEW JERSEY

Collected writings
Copyright © 2012 by Anthony Buccino, All rights reserved.

Published by Cherry Blossom Press
P.O. Box 110252
Nutley. NJ 07110
www.AnthonyBuccino.com

ISBN-13: 978-1477460542

ISBN-10: 1477460543

Second Edition 1.16

Contents previously published in *A FATHER'S PLACE - An Eclectic Collection, SISTER DRESSED ME FUNNY, RAMBLING ROUND, Inside and Outside at the Same Time*, in newspapers and online.

No part of this book may be reproduced or transmitted in any form or by any means, electronic or mechanical, including photocopying, recording, or by any information storage and retrieval system, without written permission from the copyright owner.

Dedicated to

my grandparents

Lucy and Domenic Buccino

who settled and raised a family

in Belleville, New Jersey,

nearly 100 years ago

Table of Contents

Waiting for Jerry the ice cream man
Don the TV man
The pipeline under the power lines
Rainy day children of the summer
Gary's English Racer vs. My Schwinn
Chasing the mosquito man
Air raid drill memories
Penny candy from the corner store
After the Titanic
Moving down Meacham hill
Pizza for dinner, so very rare
The first robin of spring
Bellwood Crier has-been
Summer peaches in the Rambler
Billy Newtner's bus rides
Yellow cracker school days
Selling pretzels at school football games
Job rock in prose
Peter Pan Revisited, again
Back to school, institutional green
Just another day on Police Beat
Memories of Brookdale soda
Brown bagging lunch through the years
Scouts seek nudist camp over the mountain
Bob Dylan in Belleville
Flashback, summers and Suntan Lake
No Christmas
How many hammers is enough?

A father's place
My generation
On outliving two classmates
Monk's castle joyrides
Do we ever stop missing our folks?
Married to a Christmas nut
Of Taylor ham, skorpers and Ashtabula
Who is Brother, who is Uncle Bim?
At Spatola's Home for Funerals
Strangers in old photos
Counting change
Editor imprisoned in Town Hall
School 10 students surprise Belleville scribe
Remembering Belleville 'Red Tail' pilot
Italian American roots in Belleville, Nutley
Thankful for growing up in old Belleville

Waiting for Jerry the ice cream man

Back in the day, our refrigerator's freezer was the size of two ice trays and a pound of chop meat. Then that small cool space froze over and there was NEVER room for ice cream unless it was your birthday!

It was the same way up and down the block on Gless Avenue in Belleville. Anybody who got rid of their ice box and got an electric refrigerator had about the same amount of freezer space.

Unlike an actual ice box, think: the kitchen on The Honeymooners, where you put in a block of ice and it melted water into a pail underneath, these new-fangled refrigerators used electricity to take heat and make cold.

The biggest drawback in the modern world of the 1950s, which no one thought of it as a drawback on such a modern convenience, was that crust of ice forming outside the metal casing that served as the tiny freezer.

The longer you let the fridge go between defrosting, the thicker the ice formed until you couldn't put anything on the shelf alongside the freezer.

And if you needed to get some ice cubes or, later, a frozen TV dinner out of the freezer, you needed an ice pick (or butter knife, or both) to chip through the ice pack until you unearthed the block that held your treasure.

This is Jersey. It's hot in the summer in New Jersey. We were hot. We sweated and drank tap water to cool off. We ran around in the sun, got sun burn, it peeled, and we went back out in the sun.

We made wooden swords and beat the daylights out of each other until the swords broke in pieces. Then we crawled around in the dirt, set ants on fire, and played handball in the dead end street.

There was usually someone's grandmother with her hair in a bun, a heavy black shawl sitting on a front porch when we played. We never used foul language. Most of us wouldn't have known it if we heard it.

The kids on the block went through Grade 8 at School 7 in Belleville, or Holy Family School or St. Mary's School in Nutley. Belleville High

School was still on Washington Avenue. In the summer, it was hot. We played in the heat.

Nobody on the block had air conditioning. The closest our family came was when Dad brought home a Lasko three-speed oscillating fan and put it in the living room window. All the rest of the windows were left open and the slight breeze lifted the thin curtains to shift the air in our four-room cold-water flat.

We kids kept cool by running around outside and making our own breezes. We played hide-and-seek and learned to count to 100 by fives. At our peak on that one dead end block we had up to 28 kids. (We're talking baby boom, here.)

We had one set of twins from the house across the street. They were the oldest of that brood of five. Adults had a hard time telling them apart, but to us kids Jan and Joan looked nothing alike. They were a few years older than me. The last time they played with the kids my age, probably cowboys and Indians or Army, they spotted some boys they went to school with heading our way through the fields and quickly dropped the toy guns we'd loaned them to play along saying, "We can't play with you anymore."

Denise, who lived across the street with a brother Tom and a sister Rosemary, didn't play all that much. She had some kind of heart surgery in the 1950s and we boys had to be extra gentle around her. She was a year older than me but smaller, and a whole lot prettier. Their house had a side yard with garages in the back and the girls would put together a carnival fund-raiser for some charity each year. They'd set up booths and rides and all the kids in the neighborhood would have a great time.

On hot summer nights when we heard the truck horn play "Mary Had A Little Lamb", all of us kids would rush out to "Jerry the Ice Cream Man."

We'd tell him what we want and he'd probe through the thick hatch into the freezer for the ice cream bar or ice pop of our choice. Then he'd give us our change from a change dispenser he wore on his belt.

Lon Cerame, the genuine rock and roll teenager on Gless Avenue, remembers that Jerry and his brother George had a store in Lyndhurst. It was a small food store where when Lon and his pal Dave Macaluso would ride their bikes to Teterboro Airport, they stopped in to get some water and talk to George who was running the store.

Jerry or George would come to our area after dinner time, usually after the mosquito man in the jeep would pass by to share that cloud of toxic spray we all loved to run through. We spent many hot summer nights running after the "Mosquito Man" chasing him through the sweet-smelling blue cloud of smoke emitting from his county-owned Jeep. It could kill mosquitoes but we never gave a thought as to what it could do to us.

Lon says that when Jerry would be getting an ice pop for a kid on the side of the truck, Lon would always press the button on the door in the back freezer and lock it!

When he went to help the next kid, now at the back of the truck, Jerry would always get angry when he found the freezer door locked. Now, he had to stop what he was doing to go in the truck cab, turn off the engine and get the key to unlock the freezer,

Good old Jerry never caught the wise guy. So, the more often Jerry got angry, the more often Lon sought the perfect opportunity to lock it.

Lon remembers two of his favorites from the truck, one pop called "brown cow" and the coconut vanilla pop that was really good.

My favorite was called chocolate cake, it was an ice cream bar covered with cake crumbs. Other kids liked frozen ice pops that left a mustache the color of the flavor when you were done eating it.

On our birthday, we got a free ice cream. My birthday was in June so I always got one free ice cream. Our friends born in cooler weather always missed out. Nyuk, nyuk!

Sometimes you'd hear a kid yelling up to an open window asking his mom or dad for ice cream money and they'd say, "No, we have some in the freezer."

But everybody who heard that, even the kid being denied ice cream, knew that it meant that we don't have the dime or quarter to spare for your treat.

That's how it was in our working class neighborhood, in the 1950s and 1960s.

In my new neighborhood, on Carpenter Street near School 10, no ice cream truck came through our neighborhood. The one-way street only had houses on one side for the most part, and there weren't as many kids as on my old small dead-end street.

But there was something unusual in being just slightly across town from where I spent my first ten years of life. The truck that came along sold snow cones. They were essentially crushed ice with raspberry, orange, cherry or some other juice flavored concentrate squirted over them. Then you tried to eat it so the ice and the juice lasted till the end, like that morning bowl of cereal and milk.

These new-fangled snow cones turn out to be one of the good things about moving to Bellwood, leaving behind old friends, that old parochial school and wearing uniforms to class.

Don the TV man

Don the TV Man drove a red Ford panel truck that he likely bought new in 1955 or so. In the 1960s it didn't seem so old, but by the 1990s when he was still tooling down the street, it tended to stand out against the minivans and SUVs.

It was eventually sold to a fellow in England, probably for more than Don the TV man paid for it in the mid-50s, maybe for more than Don the TV man ever made from repairing TVs. But it's early in the story and I digress.

Don the TV man was huge, stocky and huge, especially since I knew him from the time I could walk and he was already grown up. His arms were ham hocks and his fists as big as boxing gloves, and yet he handled the screwdrivers and the glass tubes without popping them like a child's floating bubble.

His hair, jet-black and slicked back, fit snugly under his beanie-like cap. He always had a cigar that he chewed but didn't smoke inside the house. And for all his bulk and talk, he was the nicest guy you could ever pick to be on your side.

He'd open up his heavy toolbox and trays upon trays of boxes of parts and test tubes in cardboard boxes shifted before him. They all said "Made In USA".

Removing the long, tiny Phillips-head screws, Don the TV man slipped off the vented cardboard backing and set it down, then fiddling with one hand in the back where glass tubes either lit up or didn't light up, wherein the problem might lie, and in his other hand, extended to the front of the set, he held a small vanity mirror to watch the screen.

When I was older, sometimes he let me hold his flashlight as he jiggled tubes, pulling some out and switching some, or turned a knob to see "what's it looks like now."

"Still rolling!" I'd shout. Or "Still full of ghosts!"

Just when you thought he had the problem licked and we could go back to watching our regularly scheduled program, Don the TV man would say, "time for a break."

Dad would leave the room, apparently in mid story, and reappear with glasses and a bottle of Scotch. Before putting the bottle or the glasses down on the table, Dad would point to the pencil mark and date on the side of the bottle from the last time Don the TV man visited.

Don the TV man would fill the shot glass and continue with his story. He knew everything, and if the job was big enough, he'd tell you everything about everybody.

He knew which politicians were crooked and all the places the mob took over, and could tell you how this guy was hooked up with that guy and how they got away with everything they did.

But Don the TV man was a working stiff. He knew he'd have to work forever because all the crooks and politicians were going to steal the Social Security and leave the honest hard-working people with nothing.

He'd talk away, and I'd nod my pre-pubescent head, mirroring my dad, as if I understood whatever he was saying about getting old and retiring.

We were always happy to get Don the TV man to fix our TV. He worked in the days before everyone had answering machines. In fact, he never answered his phone. We knew the trick to getting picked up by his repair antenna when we needed him.

Lucky for us we knew where on Gless Avenue he stored his wooden extension ladders for antenna work. We'd keep an eye out for him coming or going with the ladders. Then holler down from our second floor back porch.

Otherwise, we'd call on one of his brothers to tell Don the TV man we needed him to come by because our Motorola was acting up again.

Then, late one evening after pining for days about the rolling picture or the ghosts on Channel 2, about when we'd all but forgotten, Don the TV man would call to make sure we were home.

In those days our family never went to a store to buy a TV or hi-fi stereo, we got them from, yeah, you guessed it, Don the TV man.

And all those TVs, those beautiful, expensive black and white TVs, all came in beautiful, real wood cabinets that then were the most stylish, up-to-date article of furniture in the house. Don the TV man sold us the best stuff. My sister's hi-fidelity stereo record player from the 1960s is still spinning vinyl today, more than 50 years later.

Long after Don the TV man semi-retired, I'd still have him take a look at one of my newer sets before tossing it. He was the last resort after we tired of slapping the side of the set to get it to go back to normal. Sometimes we'd get a few more years out of it. Or he'd tell us it was shot.

Those times I'd bring it to his house and we'd sit around chewing the fat over a few cold ones. Then it would be the same when I came back to pick up the set. Over a few beers he'd tell me how he had to run around for the part they don't make anymore and how much it cost him – he couldn't believe the prices. It was always good to catch up on who the crooks were and how the country was doing.

The Ciccolini who sells me my TVs these days is pleasant enough, but it's just the brilliant picture, the tech sheet, cable, remote, the delivery schedule, and the credit card. There's no tubes, no glasses, no bottle of Scotch, and I never get to hold the flashlight anymore or say "The picture's still fuzzy!"

The pipeline under the power lines

"Hey, Ant! You got a third eye!" Gary yells but it doesn't help me see much better.

Fumbling, I pick up my twenty-six-inch Schwinn, but I drop it just as quickly. Then pick it up again. Holding it up, it's holding me up.

Gary is staring at me. I sense this more than I see it. I can't see much of anything really. Gary looks like a tree, the bike in my hand seems a tangled red bush. The world isn't spinning but it's sure coming in cloudy. I sense something tremendous has transformed my eight-year-old body.

"That's what happens when your bike hits a rock on the pipeline," Gary explains.

"And my head finds its own rock," I moan. "Man, that was great! Like flying!"

"You need to work on your landing," says Gary, my best friend, and usual partner in everything that makes growing up in the 1960s memorable.

At the end of Gless Avenue, our dead end street, a large overgrown field crosses our block like a T.

Above the fallow field, high in the sky, humming wires sagged from tower to tower, running east and west, as far as the eye could see up the hill past Passaic Avenue and down the hill towards Nutley. Joey in the corner house said the wires went all the way to Texas.

And Joey, being two years older than most of us, and way more mature in every way, would know these things about our town and the high-tension lines and about Texas, too. He was new on the block, and moved in from Montclair where he constantly reminded us that everything was bigger and better than Gless Avenue and Belleville, too.

A hundred feet or so into the field a hump like a dragon's tail rose on our right slicing the horizon into near and far, the near being our fields and the far being the freshly built houses on Sycamore Drive. The hump trailed off to our left, south to a rising mound topped by creepy looking phallic vents before the mound sank down again to cross under Chestnut Street past the bog to the Newark reservoir on Joralemon.

We called that dragon's tail the pipeline. It rose high above the field and usually offered dry passage when the fields were flooded and the worn paths we trampled through the grass were pocked with puddles and knee-deep in Jersey mud.

Nearly diagonal of the entrance from Gless Avenue straight off into the field and partially hidden in the undergrowth from a brick wall about four feet high and about six feet wide there protruded a section of heavy pipe about two feet wide in diameter extending from the stones into space about the same.

Inside the pipe it was dark and dry, and at times we took turns crawling in to it as a hiding place, but not for long for. It creeped out us non spelunkers. Even sliding in feet first no one wanted to hang out inside the pipe with the spiders, bugs and darkness for very long, or at all.

The other end of the pipe appeared on the far side of the pipeline, and our tube apparently ran under the dragon hump drawing water that came down the hill and gathered at the other side where our pipe provided a route to continue downhill.

On the stone wall side of the extruding pipe it poured out to a trickling stream where occasionally we saw a wandering frog or box turtle.

Fresh water bubbled from under the rocks and pebbles at the base of the wall. We kids trusted that water, especially after a hike through the weeds or a game of war.

Straddling the pool we stood on big rocks beside the underground fountain. Our palms together, we scooped handfuls of cool, fresh clean water to our sweaty faces and drank the transparent treat.

Spring water bubbled into that creek for years and saved us from a trip home for a cool drink many times. Then one day the big trucks came, back hoes and cranes, too.

There was a lot of noise in the field for weeks and we couldn't play there or watch whatever they were doing either. When we returned, the field and pipeline seemed virtually unchanged, but the spring was gone.

We could still race our bikes up and down the rough trail along pipeline's dragon tail, but a cool drink no longer waited on the low side of the pipeline under the power lines.

Rainy day children of the summer

The best part of being a kid on Gless Avenue in Belleville in the 1960s was having four cousins - Patsy, Tommy, Bobby and Lorraine - living next door, and about a dozen other kids all just a few houses up or down our dead end street.

For a few years, my Dad's older brother Joe lived by himself downstairs from us after Gram died. Uncle Joe was old then, to me, anyway, and had no kids of his own, as far as any of us knew. And it seemed to us as if he was already retired, or simply too worn out to work anymore.

Someone called him a babysitter once because he had a half dozen kids and me playing on his front porch. He just smiled at the babysitter remark and waved his hands in a 'suffer the little children' gesture.

Uncle Joe didn't spoil us, but he didn't cater to us. If we wanted a glass of water or a cookie, we'd have to go home to get it. But he let us make as much noise as we wanted. We could run up and down the stairs, climb on the banisters and do all other stuff that our moms would never allow.

He just sat by, ready to spring into action if one of us got hurt or something, inside a perpetual gray cloud from his unfiltered cigarettes.

Our porch was the width of Gram's house but only about six-feet wide, the entrance up a few concrete steps at the left and to the front door, with a closed in balcony that overlooked our front yard.

Over 40 years living in that house, Gram developed the front yard into one overgrown 'snowball' bush squared off by hedges, leaving little of anything to mow. She kept the grapevines and growing fields in the back yard and stayed true to her Italian youth tending them until the day she died.

Gram owned the house next door and rented the two apartments. My father's cousin Pat and my cousins lived in one of those little apartments.

Bobby, just a year older than me, and I would see what kind of trouble we could get into in those pre-school days. He reminds me now, fifty years later, that we experimented with some of my grandmother's cats. She had so many cats that she probably didn't even know how many she had.

So, Bobby says I was the brains behind taking Gram's cats to the second floor porch in the back of the house and dropping them, in turn, to see if they really landed on their feet.

At least the cats were safe when we were hanging on the front porch with Uncle Joe.

Bobby's porch next door was the width of the house, but about twice as deep as our porch. It had what passed for a front lawn, although I'm sure we kids trampled anything that ever tried to grow there. Even though their porch was bigger, we usually congregated on my smaller porch to play checkers, Chinese checkers, chess, Old Maid or just laugh at the girls trying to jump rope on the sidewalk.

Though our mothers were home all the time when we were kids, they had their chores. On Monday they washed the clothes, on Tuesday they ironed the clothes, on Wednesday they dusted and vacuumed, on Friday they washed the floor and so on. (I guess on Thursday they ate bon-bons and watched soaps?)

At noon, our moms watched their 'stories' when Love Of Life, Search For Tomorrow, Guiding Light and whatever else came on. It helped pass the time when they could watch or listen to them as they scrubbed the house and picked up after us.

So, when it rained on those summer afternoons, our moms were just as happy to have us out of the house and not in their way. Who wanted to be in the house with mom when we could be outside in the rain with our pals? Our favorite place was our front porches during a thunderstorm where we'd watch the rain pelt the bushes, branches and the banisters.

We'd take turns running from one front porch to the other just to see if we could do it without getting wet. If we got wet, which we usually did, we'd wait until we dried off and then run back in the rain to the other porch. We'd do this until the rain stopped or we had to go inside for supper.

The last time I checked, that house I left in 1964 looks a bit different. For instance, there is a grass lawn, and the front porch closed-in banister has been replaced by open spindles. Not to mention that the faux shingles the house had since they were invented have been replaced by aluminum siding and the front windows, even on the first floor, have shutters.

Grandma wouldn't recognize the place, nor the place next door with its wide-open porch. I may drive down that street some rainy summer day and see if children might be tempted to run back and forth in the rain, just for fun.

Gary's English Racer vs. my Schwinn

You wouldn't think that a kid could get into too much trouble riding his bike up and down a dead end street.

On both sides of that Gless Avenue there were about a dozen two-family houses and not all of them had kids who rode their bikes in the street, on sidewalks that lifted near big trees, or up and down smooth and bumpy driveways.

In baseball season, we took the cards of players we didn't know and used a few of mom's clothespins to make our bikes sound like motorcycles. We always had to see who could put the most cards on the fender, how much noise you could make and how long they would stay on when you raced up and down those driveways.

Gary lived in the corner house at Meacham and Gless, upstairs from his grandparents and an uncle who may have been a secret agent or something cool like that. He carried on like a spy, ignoring us kids and driving his car into the garage, scooting in the house, then getting in his car to zip somewhere to spy on someone important.

Gary, who was a month or so younger than me, had the first English Racer on the block. It was black and had very thin tires, like an English mustache, and handlebars that curled under like a Frenchman's mustache. But the weirdest thing about that foreign-made bike was that the English people put the brakes on the handlebars.

All the rest of the kids' bikes in the neighborhood had foot brakes that you stomped with your heel and skidded to a stop. And, on our bikes, you could stomp on either right or left pedal to make the wheels stop.

But on that crazy English Racer the right hand stopped the front wheel and the left handle stopped the rear wheel, or something like that. I never could remember. And stomping on the pedal did nothing but freewheel backwards.

Riding an English Racer, with its smaller seat and attached saddlebag, always had a certain Carnaby Street panache that seemed to say you were hip. The Beatles had invaded and the Rolling Stones were rocking, so it was at the vanguard of biking to roll on an English Racer.

We'd always fight over which was faster, my one-speed Schwinn with its thick tires or Gary's three-speed English Racer. His bike had a gadget on the handlebar that you could hit with your finger and it would change up the gears on the chain you pedaled to make the bike roll.

First gear was the easiest to pedal, almost too easy, because you pedaled a lot but didn't go very far. It was supposed to be good for biking up hills. Second gear was tougher than first gear, and you could really book if you put some effort into it. Third gear was the toughest. You had to work to pedal but that gave the bike more oomph and you could really put on some distance.

Give me my Schwinn with 26-inch wheels, foot brakes, wide seat, kick stand, fenders, and while it was new, in the hand grips, those streamers twirling in the draft I made when I raced along up and down Gless Avenue.

At the dead end part of our street, a staunch three-beam, striped barricade blocked cars from driving into the fields and across the pipeline that crisscrossed under the high-tension power lines. The barricade crossed at about a thirty-degree angle as did the pavement. There's a small gap where it ended and where the field started.

When we were younger, nobody was supposed to ride your bike without asking. So, when one of my cousins from next door jumped on and took my bike for a spin, he said it was okay because the battered twenty-inch maroon bike had been his before it was handed down to me.

If a cousin, or one of the older girls from across the street took my old bike and rode it to the next house's driveway and back, I was the one screaming blue murder and chasing the rider as if he or she stole it and was never going to bring it back, and it didn't matter that I wasn't riding it when he or she took it, it's my bike and nobody else can ride it unless I say so.

So, of course, one sunny afternoon, Gary and I decided to swap bikes for a turn up and down the block. He'd ride my Schwinn and I'd ride his English racer. We'd go from his house at one end to the barricade, turn around and come back and we'd see who was fastest.

We were off! I kicked his racer into second gear and pushed my way down the street. Gary wrestled my monster rig and gave it all he had to race me, neck and neck, to the end of the street and back. We dodged parked cars, and little kids running out to see what was causing the blur of shadows whisking in the breeze.

And when we got to the last house before the barricade, Gary slowed down and began his turn around.

I stomped on the pedals and they just spun backwards, not slowing Gary's English racer or myself down one bit, as the bike raced to the barricade. It took all I could do not to panic, but I screamed like crazy and used all new words to describe Gary stupid brakes that didn't work.

I managed to steer his bike to the end of the barricade and crash into the end of the curb and land unceremoniously in the weeds.

Gary checked out his bike. It was okay. I brushed off the grass and rubbed the sting out of the parts of my body that landed firs. I was okay. I took back my bike and Gary took back his. We'd finish that race some other day.

Chasing the mosquito man

I saw the greatest minds of my dead end street running into the blue mist of the sweet-smelling cloud behind the Essex County Mosquito Man's Jeep.

Summer in the 1960s, and the living was good.

Sticky fly paper hung over the Maytag wringer washing machine next to the kitchen sink. Melmac cups were neatly stored on the yellow contact paper on the shelves behind the glass doors. Sometimes, you'd bug Ma while she was cooking and get to eat a raw hot dog. It was just like rolled baloney from Prosperi's around the corner store.

It was best to be a kid on those hot days. Butterflies flew in on their magic carpet colored wings and lit on the damp clothes on the back yard line.

Some days you found red ants in the cracks of the sidewalk. You could watch them for hours. Or stomp them. Other days you watched black ants carrying crumbs off to a hole in the pavement. Sometime you tried to get a war going between the red and the black ants.

Then Grandma came out with the pot of boiling water and you watched the ants float away.

On hot July nights, besides world famous New Jersey heat and humidity, you could count on mosquito bites and fireflies in the night.

For all the DDT -- Drop Dead Twice -- sprayed on hot summer evenings, the killer fog never seemed to eradicate mosquitoes (or lightning bugs). One always managed to squirm through a tiny hole in the metal screen and spend most of the night buzzing your ear. Remember how you hid under the sheet until you fell asleep, the buzzing drifting away in the darkness?

You could never find a mosquito truck when you need one.

On our dead end street we kids stayed out as late as we could. We played hide and seek or if we had a big ball, we played Sputnik. We'd come in and pour the calamine lotion on the bug bite welts. The rich families on the block had a window fan or two. The rest of us awaited a summer breeze through the window screen and the gossamer curtains.

We probably had the same cycle of boom and bust years for critters then as now, but, frankly, there weren't nearly so many houses in our suburbia. The critters had their place and we had ours. Who would have known if there were a lot of bunnies running around? Our cats ran the night and dogs wandered the day. Critters steered clear in those days.

This year, in our suburban town north of Newark, we've seen a lot of bunnies, chipmunks and squirrels. Some years we run into a lot of raccoons or skunks. We'd rather run into bunnies than skunks. Too bad there isn't a Mosquito Man for skunks.

I wonder where the critters go in their off years, and what calls them back in those great numbers when they are on.

It must be a lot like the lightning bug. Around here we only see them in June and July. They light up fields and back yards in summer with their private fireworks.

Kids will always chase and catch fireflies. For bugs, they fly darn slow. And low. They fly darn low, low enough for a child to reach up and catch them or watch in wonder as they alight on a tiny hand or finger.

Last month Ask Marilyn, in the Sunday Parade, wrote about fireflies. Marilyn vos Savant took the wonder out of the insects by explaining where they come from and where they go. The short answer is, the light thing, it has to do with mating, in case you didn't know.

Why is it always a little boy somewhere whose sole desire is to see what makes the little bug light up? Boys always take apart their toys to see their guts and what makes them run. Why can't they just catch them and put them in a jar with some pulled grass, and a wax paper lid, and watch them light and go dark until the sandman arrives? Those bugs were usually dead by morning light.

These days, the mosquito commission uses whirlybirds to spray swaths of bug killer over a city. Meanwhile, smart fireflies keep moving to the country. They keep finding the country is further and further away.

Now, when we see fireflies on summer nights, it seems to say we are no closer to dousing that little light of theirs than we are to clearing the bog of mosquitoes.

As man has proven himself an inept caretaker of the earth, so far, the earth has rebounded. With each round, it seems the mosquitoes get stronger and more resistant. Someday we'll look out our window from our air conditioned house and see a mosquito as big as a jetliner.

Someday the species you'll see only in a book will be man.

Air raid drill memories

When we heard the school bell ring its special ring - different than a fire drill ring or dismissal bell - we sprang into action from our desks.

Teacher calmly reminded us it was an air raid drill, "Form two lines," she barked sternly. We obliged, filing out the doorway.

In the hallways our long neat rows would have shown those Russians. Our lines were the best in the world. We marched proudly in the corridor and filed into the gymnasium.

Quickly and quietly we lined up, then, even though we were in our good school clothes, we lowered onto the floor assuming the air raid drill position.

We had our left forearm under our forehead and our right arm over the back of our head with a hand over our ear to muffle the sound of the end of the world.

From the hallway entrance to the gymnasium we must have looked like so many neat rows of Lincoln Logs.

We were lying on the floor as the rest of the school filed in to fill out the gym floor. The older grades lined up against the cold tile walls and metal lockers built into the walls.

We took cover in neat order in virtually any place that was away from the windows. We sneaked a look back and waited for the Russian's A-bomb to come crashing through any one of the many windows in our school.

Oh, why, we wondered, did they have so many windows in this school building? We could have a much better chance of survival in a nuclear holocaust if only our school had no windows.

Without any windows, we'd be way ahead of all the other schools in America. Then we could rule the world after the war, we reasoned.

The littlest of the children did not leave their classrooms at all, they simply took cover under the extensive protection of the wooden surface of their class desks.

All the while we headed for and assumed our position for the air raid, the air raid signal clanked and clanked heightening our sense of emergency.

Air raid drills were rote, as common in those days as fire drills and spelling tests on Wednesday. We took it in stride in the natural order of the day.

It was the test of the Emergency Broadcast System on our Good Guys radio station or during our afternoon game shows that irked us more.

After all, the TV and radio tests came on our own time. Plus, they interrupted our Top 40 or a favorite show.

At the beginning of the EBS test they told us, "This is a test. This is only a test." Then the TV screen went to a 'test' screen and all we heard from either medium was a boop tone.

In about a minute, it was over. They reminded us "This is a test. This is only a test. Had this been a real emergency, you would have been told where to tune for further instructions."

We passed the EBS test. All was well with the world. No emergency, neither hurricane nor Russian bombers, nor Intercontinental Ballistic Missiles were heading our way. It was back to our regularly scheduled program.

What irked us most about being distracted by a test of the EBS was that sometimes they returned us to our show which was "already in progress" so we had to think for another minute to figure out what we might have missed.

In those days the radio dial had a triangle in the number, it was called a Conelrad, that was supposed to be where we would tune in our transistor radios and know where to take cover if the Russians decided to attack after we got home from school.

Some of us, and I won't mention any names, used to leave their homework until the last minute. They figured there was no use in doing homework tonight if the world was going to be over by morning.

Before I started school in the last year of the 50s Cold War, the older kids reported being issued high-heat resistant dog tags with their names and addresses. They had to wear them at all times.

Penny candy from the corner store

It is a truth universally acknowledged that a child, after a long day of school work, must be in want of penny candy from the corner store.

Growing up, it seemed that every neighborhood from Belleville and Nutley to Bloomfield and Montclair, New Jersey all the way to Ashtabula, Ohio, and beyond had a candy store within a block of every school. Some candy stores also sold bread, cold cuts and popsicles but most of the mom and pop stores sold a variety of penny candies and other knick-knacks, doodads, and ding-a-lings the kids loved.

Baseball and football cards topped the list, of course, for the guys. And there was a time when all any boy or girl wanted to buy was Beatles trading cards. The package held five cards and a stale piece of bubblegum. If you collected enough cards in the right set, you could put together a jigsaw puzzle by turning them over. (We'd all be millionaires if our moms hadn't thrown away all that "junk".)

We had a candy store, Silac's, on the corner of my dead end street at Gless Avenue and Meacham Street in Belleville. That's all I remember of the name because it closed when I was about five or six years old. But for me, Silac's might as well have been a three-story candy store for all the treasures it held. In reality, the store was carved out of what would be the next owner's living room.

I checked in with Lon Cerame, who is a few years older than I am and lived across the street. "Who could ever forget Silac's corner store. Located on famous Gless Avenue...," he says. I think it's only famous because he and I lived there at the same time and we didn't blow up the world, but that's another story.

"Ann Silac and her husband, who was always smoking a cigarette with a holder, owned the place. But I used to see more of her than him," says Lon. "I remember her husband but can't remember his first name.

"All the candy was a penny and the more expensive stuff was only a nickel. Her kitchen was right off the store so she can see people as they walked in. To enter, you had to go up a few stairs on the front. As you opened the door, a bell would ring once telling her that someone was in the store. The candy cabinet was to the right, actually in the front of the store and her deli section was to the left. In back were all the dry goods. They had a Coke machine and I remember the iceman bringing ice which would last about a week. Then he would come back.

"Empty bottle cases were in front of the soda machine and if you brought in any empty bottles, she would give you two cents per bottle.

"I remember when I used to walk in, and before she would come out of the kitchen, I would be laying down a case of empty bottles making believe I had just brought them in. All I did was pick up the empty case and as she walked out, set it down on top of the rest, in which she would give me 24 cents." Cerame still laughs at his little joke.

"Her deli section was filled with ham, which sold for 75 cents a pound, and with other cold cuts," he recalls. "She had a daughter that owned a big farm somewhere who would bring her fresh eggs to sell."

Reprising his mischievous youth, Cerame says, "I used to walk in her store, grab candy and pay with play money and run out. She would get mad and walk over to my house and my mother would pay her!"

"Silac would close around 7 P.M. at night when the ice cream man came around in the summer."

Around the corner, on Harrison Street, between Gless and Entwistle avenues, was our fallback candy store Bill-Tone's. It was where a lot of the older Holy Family School kids went and bought lunch instead of brown bagging it or going home.

But for my friends and me, we walked in the store, past the butcher and cold cuts counter, and headed immediately for the back room where the candy counter held Circus Peanuts, candy cigarettes, wax bottles of unknown fluids, wax lips, candy bracelets, NECCO wafers, chewing gum and Mary Jane candy, of course, and Peanut Chews.

Lon remembers Chris' Cozy Corner from the 1950s and 1960s. "Chris and his wife Amanda owned it and it was on the corner of Franklin Avenue and

Harrison Street near Booth Park. It was a great place. Everyone would hang there. I know I did.

"It wasn't that big but inside there was a soda counter. Chris served light foods, nothing big. When you walked in, to the front of you was a table with all kinds of toys on it, they sold. Small cars, small trucks and all that other junk kids loved so much.

"To your right he had a magazine stand with all the latest comics and monster books from the TV and movie shows. To the left, the counter had nine seats. Near the register he had a candy stand. Every time I went there I would order the same drink, grape with water, no ice."

Lon says he was in Cozy Corner so much that fifty years later, "I can still see Chris and his wife."

In Belleville, School 7 kids living on Baldwin Place and the reservoir side of Joralemon Street went to Paganelli's, the corner store at Dawson Street and Garden Avenue for bread, cold cuts and treats like popsicles and Coke during the summer. But after school they went to Rosebud's Sweet Shop for stuff like gum and snow cones.

School 8 kids had Watter's Dairy, or Marbach's, and warm weather brought everybody from all over town to Jackie's Italian ice stand. School 3 kids met at Harriet's. School 4 kids had Zeps at Heckel and Lawrence streets.

In summer, kids from my block marched down Meacham Street to the bottom of the hill and around the corner to Shubach's where we bought what we called punks that we'd set on fire so the smoke would keep the mosquitos away.

On Saturdays and during the summer, when we visited my cousins on N. 17th Street in Bloomfield, it was always a treat to walk to First Avenue and over two blocks to cross the street where we'd visit John and Minnie's Candy Store at N. 15th and First.

That store had ice cream bars in a freezer and we'd each get to pick one out. Whichever cousin was oldest got to pay with the money we got to get out of the house. Then, we'd see who could finish theirs first before it melted or we got back to the house.

When I moved crosstown to Carpenter Street, there was Harry's Belwood Sweet Shop where all the School 10 kids could stock up on candy the teachers would confiscate if they caught you eating in class. Before it was Harry's someone tells me it was called Chet's.

In high school I stopped at Rosebud's to pick up a Wall Street Journal to read during study hall. Little would anyone then have suspected that 30 years later I'd be proofreading stories for the paper.

As soon as I got my driver's license I started dating a girl from Orange. As I was plotting how to get there, driving mom's single overhead cam Pontiac Tempest, on the Parkway, Ma pointed out a back roads way through Bloomfield where I wouldn't be taking her car on the super highway.

Cathy lived on Chapel Street in Orange across the street from St. John's Cemetery and the catholic school. Her family lived upstairs from the candy store at the street level. It reminded me of the family grocery store on The Many Loves of Dobie Gillis, a popular TV show from when I was a kid. We only dated long enough for her to point out that she knew all the people who carved their initials on the trees in the woods at Eagle Rock Reservation.

I never got a chance to prance in the candy aisles, like Veruca Salt in Willy Wonka, and pick treats to satisfy my sweet tooth cravings. Nor did I carve initials in a tree trunk.

I did, however, wheel into Harry's for a consolation chocolate shake and a grab bag of penny candies.

After the Titanic

When the Titanic sank in April 1914, my grandparents had already made their frightening voyage across the Atlantic from Laviano in Southern Italy. They brought along their four children, and my grandfather set out to earn a living as a common laborer. My grandmother tended the vegetable gardens providing food for the growing family.

By the 1920s they bought a house and property in a rural community in northern New Jersey, a few miles west of the Statue of Liberty, in a place with a French name that reminded them of their native farmland, a place called Belleville.

They had settled in an area of the town called Guinea Hill, now known as Passaic Avenue. Many of their relatives settled nearby, some were in Belleville, others in Nutley. A visit to share the wine and speak their native tongue was usually a short walk on a dirt road.

In 1925 along came the power company to purchase the family's property which was in the way of the new power lines. Since the utility only wanted the land, my grandparents moved the house, literally with a horse and wagon, to some new property down the hill next to another house grandpa and his compares had built on a dirt road called Gless Avenue. There, the neighbors were few and my grandparents set up their farm with goats, chickens, a vegetable garden and the all-important grapevines.

Both of grandpa's houses had cellars with low ceilings. Here he stored the wine presses and barrels. High clearance in a basement would not be needed for at least two generations when the prosperous influence of the new land produced taller children. For now, the basements provided space for the coal bins and the cool storage of provisions, and, of course the dark, strong home-made wine.

Dad's half-sister was a teenager when she came to America. Her mother had died and my grandfather had married my grandmother. Shortly after they came to this country, my aunt Assunta married and began her family. Before long she had children who were older than her new half-siblings. Aunt 'Sue' and her family lived in a three-room cold water flat on 5th Street in Newark. Her children were visited often by Grandpa Domenic with his horse and wagon. He took them for rides around the block and gave them each a nickel before he left.

As a matter of perspective, Susie's children thought our grandparents were rich. An older cousin told me, "Grandpa and grandma had good food to eat. And there was food available all the time, and they lived in a big house with a big, big yard and we could run as much as we liked and not worry about getting run over. And when we left, we carried bags of vegetables from the garden and fruit from the trees" from Grandpa's farm in the country called Belleville.

Life in the new country was good. My grandparents had two more children born in America. Their American farm was just about the only house on the hill. In Belleville, they had found a place where they could nearly live as the simple farm folk as in the old country.

Grandma harvested the vegetables, figs, pears, grapes and eggs. Her American farm seemed to stretch out forever although it was barely a hundred feet in any direction. Through the grapevines no houses could be seen on the next block. The goats provided milk for the children, and the chickens' fresh eggs and more. On Sunday she would select a chicken, lop off its head, drain it in a sink, then cook it, smother it in fresh tomato gravy and serve the family.

With few other skills besides farming, no mastery of the language of the new country, my grandfather supported his growing family with the meager rent of the extra house and by working as a common laborer. It was after a stint of digging ditches that on Feb. 4, 1929, my grandfather died of pneumonia. He left behind five young children on the precipice of what would become the new nation's economic nightmare.

Throughout the Great Depression and beyond, Grandma survived. She had her 'rents' coming in, and her farm was full of fresh food in the dead end street. The back porch railings were flush with tomatoes, peppers, and gourds set to dry in the sun. Her children went to School 7 and assimilated into the 'Mitigan' culture and learned its language and customs.

When the boys were older, they worked for the town to pay the taxes on the family house. Later, they found work with the CCC and other work projects of the Great Depression. About the time the work projects were ending, along came World War II and so many of these first generation boys joined the service to fight for the country that had held such hope for their parents.

Post-war found more houses on Gless Avenue A mini-U.N. had developed on our block with families speaking Polish, Italian or Greek. The old women and old men spoke to each other in their native, yet different, tongues and somehow seemed to understand each other. All their children spoke the language of the new land.

My parents spent a generation becoming Americanized, trying to leave behind their parents' ties to the customs and language of Southern Italy. After all, they had fled the old country because to stay would have meant continued hardship, poverty and destitution. In America there was a chance to earn a living, own a piece of land and more than merely survive.

In the early part of this century the thing to do was blend in with the 'Mitigans.' My ancestors struggled to learn the new language and assimilate their children in schools. At home and with their compares, they spoke their native dialect. My father hadn't spoken English until he started school. My parents rarely talked their ancestors' language, when they did, it was only to confound little ears that would be better off not knowing what was being discussed.

By the middle of this century, when I came along, it seemed that only the very old relatives spoke Italian. Therefore, we youngsters assured ourselves that when we got old, in our 80s or 90s like the relatives we saw around us, we too would speak Italian. We wouldn't have to take lessons, it would come naturally, we knew it for sure. Except for several brief lessons from our second grade nun at Holy Family School, no one ever tried to teach us more than good morning and good afternoon in our native tongue. Throughout every classroom in that school most of the children's last names ended in a vowel and their grandparents or parents had settled in Belleville and Nutley from Southern Italy. These children had become Americanized. Few of their parents spoke Italian at home. None of the children spoke it at school. To the pleasure and hope of our ancestors who left certain destitution, these descendants had become 'Mitigans' and would always know prosperity among these amber waves of grain.

In the 1950s and 1960s the second generation enjoyed the fruits of our ancestors' sacrifices. I grew up in the house my grandfather built more than 30 years earlier. By today's standards, it was a crude shelter, a four-room cold-water flat. The house was warmed by two coal furnaces. I remember the noise of the coal crashing down the chute into the coal bin. I gazed in mystical wonder watching my dad stoke the glowing coals. He had mastered the art of how much coal to stoke to keep the house warm at night.

On bath night, my mom broke out the spaghetti pots, filled them with water and set them on the gas stove. Later she mixed them in the tub with cold water from the tap. We children thought this not unusual, we knew nothing any different. Each Christmas, there was a decorated tree and presents beneath. What more could we ask from our loving parents? Life, as far as we could see it in America, was good.

Summer nights on our dead end street we kids played until the mosquitoes came out. One game we played based on dodge ball was "SPUTNIK" where each child took a letter from the word and had to get the ball if his letter was called. We also played hide 'n seek, and counted by fives to a hundred as the others hid. In the fields at the end of our dead end street, the continuation of the fields where my grandparents had their first house, underneath the power lines, we boys played War and variously won out over Japan or Germany. We rode our bicycles along the water pipeline, and sometimes, when the grass was not too high, we played baseball in the fields.

Taking a break from the heat, we awaited the sound of a truck horn playing "Mary Had A Little Lamb" and knew that "Jerry the ice cream man" would be along soon. We'd call out our requests and he'd reach his arm into the small doors of his ice cream truck and bring out our favorite ice pops. Later, when the sun went down, we awaited the arrival of the "Mosquito Man." He wasn't a giant bug or a super hero. He was an employee of the county who drove a Jeep up and down our street. On the back of his Jeep he had a smoke machine that emitted bug spray to kill the mosquitoes. All the kids in my neighborhood ran yelling, laughing and coughing in the sweet-smelling cloud of DDT behind the Jeep.

The most memorable moments of the summer came after dark on July 4. After a dinner where many relatives had gathered we headed into the street. We kids, mostly grandchildren of immigrants from Italy, Poland and Greece gathered at the railing that blocked our dead end street from the field. We faced south and quickly turned west on cue. The older kids warned us where to watch so we could see the fireworks displays from Belleville, Bloomfield, and East Orange. In the distance we saw the bursts and heard the booms signaling freedom in the only land we had ever known as home.

In the dead end street, this generation was blissfully unaware of the sacrifices and hardships endured few decades earlier so they could stand, without hunger, without persecution, among a mix of nationalities making up the boiling pot of the land called America where they could all enjoy the same freedom of opportunity to go anywhere and become anything. Not until decades hence would these children sense the peril our ancestors endured to give us a chance at a better life as a 'Mitigan.'

Moving down Meacham hill

When my grandparents moved from Passaic Avenue half way down the hill to Gless Avenue, they literally moved the house down the hill. In the 1920s or so, when the electric company decided it wanted to run power lines across Belleville, my grandparents' house was in the path. It, and they, had to go.

According to family legend, Grandpa Domenic and Grandma Lucy sold their lot to the electric company which had no use for the actual house (or perhaps, houses) sitting on the land. My grandfather enlisted their compares, many horses and logs and somehow literally moved the building(s) to the spot in the dead end street where our family lived until 1964.

To their advantage, many of Grandma's relatives lived within a short walk. One could always count on a cousin, aunt, uncle or countryman to be passing nearby and always ready to lend a hand, especially when it was wine tasting time.

Compares owned the few houses and most of the open land from Harrison Street to Meacham. Another *paisan* once owned the land that houses Holy Family School, rectory and church.

In that neighborhood, every open dirt patch became a garden and in season you could see fig and pear trees rising, six-foot tall yellow sunflowers, large dark leaves hiding cucumbers, vegetables growing everywhere and lush grapevine arbors sucking in New Jersey sunshine and practically hear the dark grapes plumping.

There, on that hill, Grandpa Domenic and Grandma Lucy lived among kin as in a village as near as could be to life among their farm folk in Laviano, Italy. The only exception was the poverty they left behind. It helped that most of the Italians in the neighborhood spoke the same dialect along and wondered at what little English their children brought home from school.

In our family history, the name of Grandpa's first wife has been lost. She bore him at least one daughter, Assunta, and then died in Italy. Grandpa married Lucy and she bore him more children before and after they came to America in 1914 or so. Susie married in 1916 at Holy Family Church, her first child was older than some of her half-siblings.

Susie settled her family in a three-room cold-water flat on the fourth floor, front, on Fifth Street in Newark, remembers her daughter Marie. A year younger than the author's father, Cousin Marie remembers that her mother often sent her children to grandma's house to spend time in the country wilderness that was Gless Avenue in Belleville.

Grandma's farm was just about the only house on the hill and their green farmland stretching as far as the eye could see. Susie's seven children thought their grandparents rich because they always "had good food to eat and there was food available all the time and they lived in a big house with a big, big yard and we could run as much as we liked and not worry about getting run over and no one seemed angry."

Cousin Marie remembers, "When we left, we carried bags of vegetables from the garden and fruit from the trees" from Grandpa's farm. "It was so bountiful and grandma was so loving and treated us real good."

In her childhood Cousin Marie remembers there was only one other house on Gless Avenue. Grandma owned all the property and the farm took up the whole block. She says Grandma was loving but not a good housekeeper, preferring the outdoors, her garden and her animals.

For Sunday dinner, Grandma lopped the head off a chicken and hung it to drain in the sink, and then she cooked it and served it with fresh garden tomato gravy.

Cousin Marie drew water from one of two deep, round, stone-rimmed wells using wooden buckets held in place by a thick clothes line. A dipper was always handy for a cool drink.

Grandpa Domenic built a shed and he worked in the back yard where they grew vegetables galore and raised chickens, pigs and had a cow, too. Grandpa enjoyed those visits from Susie and her family. The children grew to love his bald head, his light but ruddy complexion and bright blue eyes. In turn, Grandpa Domenic visited them in Newark with his horse and wagon. He took them for rides around the block and gave each child a nickel before he left.

On February 4, 1929, Grandpa Domenic died of pneumonia at age 59. He left his wife and children, Connie, Dottie, Joe, Angelo and Val.

Through the Depression and long after, Grandma had rents coming in from the second floor and the house next door, but she lost her property in Nutley to back taxes.

In the beautiful village her "farm" overflowed with fresh grown food, while chickens and goats wandered about while she tended her beloved grape vines. On railings of the open-air back porch the sun dried her tomatoes, peppers, and gourds.

As soon as they were old enough, the boys went off into the Works Progress Administration, or WPA, and worked on projects in the Civilian Conservation Corps, CCC. Later, the younger boys were drafted and the oldest was rejected from service because he had been born in Italy. Meanwhile, Grandma made due on her small patch of earth on a hillside in Belleville and waited for word from her boys overseas.

Pizza for dinner, so very rare

A long, long time ago, in the place where you live now, the children and most families who lived here knew the traditional pizza pie as a rare and luxurious treat. Dad arriving home with a hot pizza pie to surprise the family was like setting up a Christmas tree in your living room in July.

In the 1950s and 1960s, many families had one working parent and most moms stayed home to take care of the house and raise their family. We called them housewives because most often in those days, the men went to work and the women did the housekeeping chores.

Going out to dinner in those days usually followed a raise at work, an anniversary or ma's birthday. If we went anywhere it was usually Rutt's Hut or some long-gone place my parents favored.

Most times Ma cooked everything we ate. In our household that meant usually meat and potatoes or something Italian with gravy and Italian bread. When dad went out to dinner, he usually treated himself to a steak, it being one of the foods he missed most while serving in Guadalcanal and the South Pacific during World War II.

Taking the family out for pizza in those days was rare in my working class family. Dad, a union carpenter, often faced months of unemployment depending on the economy and construction industry. There wasn't a lot of money to spend at restaurants or pizzerias.

In the beginning, I only knew one kind of pizza. It was the round pie-shaped dough with melted mozzarella cheese and tomato sauce on it. Dad called them *"la petes"* or a tomato pie. All I could ever remember was pizza pie and that was all I ever really wanted to eat.

We always had a case or two of Brookdale soda in our house, and we poured it freely to wash down those hot, tasty slices.

The only topping that turned up on our pizzas in those days was *alice* (pronounced ah leege), those very salty, fishy tasting anchovies which were anathema to a child's palate.

I'd turn up my nose to any pizza with anchovy. It was worse than drinking club soda or that quinine water my dad kept around.

We kids never heard of toppings in those days. You wanted pepperoni, you got the stick of pepperoni from the fridge, a sharp knife and the box of Ritz crackers and you ate your pepperoni.

Olives? Olives were something Ma kept in a can for the fancy parties which were few and far between. We'd rather snack on the leftover pignoli nuts. Peppers on a pizza? Really, that's something only a grown-up would eat.

As for folks who suggest sausage or meatballs on a pizza, well, the only place for sausage and meatballs is in the Sunday gravy.

It was one New Year's Eve when our family was invited to a party where George De Lizio's mother, or maybe his grandmother, would make her home made pizza for everyone.

Well, she may not have spoken any English but she translated my plain old ordinary pizza tastes to a new style that we would later identify as Sicilian or a deep-dish pie. I was converted, and yet, disappointed that it might be another year before we were invited back for more.

Fortunately, by the time the late 1960s came, things had progressed where I could stay home on a Friday night and order a pizza delivered. I never minded being home alone because I had my TV shows planned and my food, too.

As soon as Gomer Pyle U.S.M.C. came on, I'd call the local pizzeria, Paddle Pizza on Belleville Avenue across the border in Bloomfield, and my pie would arrive by the time Hogan's Heroes was underway. My favorite came from a long-gone place called Lou's Pizza Pit.

Sometimes there'd be a slice or two left over and Mom would eat it when she got in from Bingo. Most times there was just an empty box.

These days when I allow myself a slice or two of modern pizza, the spices and flavor take me back to that house on Gless Avenue in Belleville, New Jersey, where I first tasted that exotic treat and my sister and my parents feasted with big smiles all around. And then to those pubescent years when a Friday night pizza was the harbinger of two days off.

Perhaps that's why pizza has become a staple menu item these days, as youngsters like me have grown into the folks who make the dining decisions and eating pizza – even if it's every day, or three times a day – still can feel like a special treat, a comforting food in uncomfortable times.

The first robin of spring

The only house my parents ever owned in Belleville was on Carpenter Street, a narrow, one-way north street, from Belleville Avenue to Continental Avenue, with houses on the left side and on the right, behind a barb-wire topped six-foot fence, grassy fields and a few rolling hills led to the iconic Isolation Hospital with the Verdigris peaked roof visible from tall mountains far, far away, and the private golf course across the valley in Bloomfield.

The south end of the street had a brick house on the right hand side, before the grounds swept up to the hospital. Then the fence started. On the right, came a few late model single family houses, then two sets of garden apartments on Carpenter Terrace South and then Carpenter Terrace North.

We lived beyond the apartments, in the eighth house (at the time) on the left.

Our immediate neighbor to the south lived in a house set back a long way from the street and had its front obscured by prize-winning mimosa trees and a thick, overgrown hedge. Most drivers who were looking for that house almost always drove by and had to back up against the one-way when they saw our house. That house was also the bane of mailmen as the two story bungalow was at the far end of a dirt driveway that turned to muddy troughs in inclement weather.

Between the hidden bungalow next door and our red and gray house, we owned a long slender lot that stretched back more than two-hundred feet to our neighbors on Fairway, and added to the park-like setting of our Hermitage. When we looked across the street we saw the wide open field, then a distant copse of pine trees before the berm obliterating any sense of the busy cars rushing along Franklin Avenue.

That barb wire topped six-foot fence deterred most trespassers, but we kids dug a hole, here or there and scooted under the hard sharp wires whenever we wanted to play football, field hockey or homerun derby.

At the far end of our yard, behind the oversized garage was an abandoned chicken coop. My dad tore down the wooden structure and left the old stone block foundation just in case he wanted to put up a pigeon coop at that site. But because our yard held the largest garage you ever saw in a private yard – it was big enough to store at least a dozen cars – it blocked any view of the coop that would have stood behind it had my carpenter dad decided to build there.

My dad was big on birds. He loved his pedigree homing pigeons. On Carpenter Street, we always had two trays of water fresh and available for the wild birds. And mom always saved the bread loaf ends to toss out to the birds that gathered in our black walnut and mimosa trees, and the various rose and what-not bushes that ran along the property line between our house and the bungalow next door.

From the time he was a whirling dervish and into young manhood, dad had homing pigeons. When he was overseas during World War Two and got leave in Australia, he walked the neighborhoods scouting out their pigeon coops. So, one of his main reasons for buying the home on Carpenter Street was its location – for the homing pigeons. With two golf courses to the east and west and the hospital grounds across the street, his birds would have been hard-pressed to find a reason to miss their coop when coming home from a race.

A corner of the garage was converted into a pigeon coop and the water troughs filled for the wild birds that gathered to eat our cast off bread, and we sat as specks on the giant lawn that took more than an hour to mow each week, enjoying the prettyish kind of wilderness. And one day in our first spring in that new home on Carpenter Street, under our giant walnut tree one day appeared a baby robin which is where this story begins.

Our side yard on Carpenter Street had plenty of trees, mimosas and black walnut mostly. The former blossom pretty pink flowers when they are ready. The black walnut trees drop golf ball sized nuts with their coarse, thick green skins, apparently to ease their landing.

The padded coating comes in handy when a walnut – or a bunch of walnuts on stem – drops 50 feed and lands on your head. It's embarrassing, and stings for a while, but leaves nothing longer lasting than a green skid mark on your head, and perhaps a little bump.

Step out the side door into the lot and there's that big black walnut tree. It served as the base for Ma's clothesline that ran out through the air to the far mimosa in the center of the side lot and looped back again.

One day, under that tall black walnut tree we found a baby robin on the ground. Perhaps a storm blew by and whisked it out of the nest. Or a squirrel shook the branch, or perhaps some green black walnut hit the nest and trampolined the bird in to the sky sending the ball of fluff through the air – a bit ahead of schedule – to land unceremoniously on the soft pile of grass clippings.

The robin was young, very young and frail, but not so frail that we couldn't pick it up and transfer it to a spare canary cage and tend to the bird, proffering it milk-soaked bread from an eye dropper.

So, that was my job, feeding the little bird, and I shared the job with whoever else was around, mom, dad or my teenaged sister. We could have pretended we were all living on a farm. We all looked after the wild helpless little robin as it grew stronger and flew from perch to perch building its wing muscles while railing against the cruel and unwarranted imprisonment behind these chrome bars.

After growing up with dad's homing pigeons, picking up and gently holding a robin was really nothing, like holding a handful of soft, scared, sacred air.

This would have made a great science project for Mrs. James Fifth Grade class at School 10 where I barely squeaked by, she said, after I learned everything wrong in my old parochial school.

Heck, I wasn't used to picking out clothes to wear to school every day instead of my tie and uniform and she expected me to remember everything that was drilled into my head by the habited ones. Leaving that old school was a lot like being paroled. I had a new life in a new house. I could make new friends and the first thing I did was forget what went before. In September, I entered Fifth Grade after the tabula rasa summer of 1964.

What would I know about a science project? How's this: If you're really good all your life, when you die, you get to live again? That should have been my Fifth Grade science report. Instead, I took some scrap wood from the giant garage, tapped in some finishing nails and strung some rubber bands from nail to nail and called it an instrument.

Picture a Charles Brown Christmas tree as a science project. Got that picture in your head? His tree would have been an A-plus next to my scrap of wood.

At the science fair where we all got to show off our science projects, the kid down the block had created a real volcano that exploded and shot out sparks and lava. I had a cast-off piece of window moulding with big brads sticking out catching on everything and anyone who walked too closely by, topped by rubber bands stretched out to the max and about to snap when you least expect it.

"Can you play a tune on that thing, Anthony?"

"No, ma'am, I don't know music," I said flatly.

Maybe if I had more time to work on the project? You can be sure the teacher told us the night before that the project was due, so, that's when I did it.

Don't go taking the teacher's side that she told us weeks and months ahead of the due date. (This is my flashback aside, and I'll tell it the way I remember it. You'll have to make up your own stories.) I'm sure she told us the afternoon before, "Don't forget, children, your science projects are due tomorrow."

In retrospect, if I had the foresight to show I could save one wild, red-breasted robin, then I might have been able to bring up my science grade and gone on to become a famous scientist instead of you-know-what.

The little bird and I got along well. I think it was happy to see me – not that you could see it smile, it was happy to see me in the same was it was happy our dog Butch didn't eat it when I held it to his nose for a sniff.

And that feathered critter helped me get to know some of the neighborhood kids. They all came by at one time or another to check out my little charge flitting from perch to perch in the spare canary cage.

If I ever did a science project, I would have stood in front of the class and said how we fed the gossamer waif. Yes, we soaked bread in milk and at first had to feed it with an eye-dropper. It was just like in those cartoons we all watched, with its mouth as wide as a steam shovel bucket and twice as hungry. But as the North American Robin (Turdus migratorius) is a migratory songbird of the thrush got bigger, we disposed of the dropper and fed it small clumps of soggy bread.

Then we worked up to some of the small seeds from dad's pigeon feed and bits of earth worm. Of all that we fed the baby bird, the worms were the weirdest. They were skin on the outside and dirt on the inside. At least the soggy milk-bread reminded us of something we might eat ourselves, like our morning sugar frosted flakes.

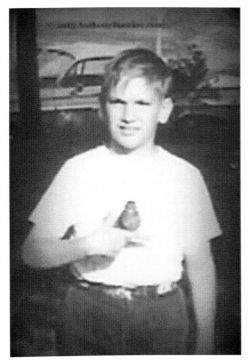

One day when the robin was stronger and its angel hair down cover given over to fine feathers, I released it from the cage and watched it soar and zip and climb and land on a shelf here, the wooden Brookdale soda crate over there on our screened-in porch.

It liked that. It wasn't all that interested in flying to my outstretched finger. But I had him again and my mom got the camera to take a photo of me and my bird under the tree where we found it.

I settled it and kept it calm, and held my hand out as Mom snapped the Kodak.

The bird flew to a low hanging branch in the black walnut tree. I stuck out my finger and waited as if it was a trained falcon like on Disney. The robin didn't come to me, so I whistled, held my hand out higher and eyed the robin in the branch just out of reach. It watched me back.

At last, the red breasted robin left its branch, flying towards me, then shot straight up winging over my head leaving a white wet chalk mark on my forehead, disappearing forever into the back pages of a young boy.

Bellwood Crier has-been

Over the summer of 1964 I had forgotten how to spell. This became painfully aware to me when my new fifth grade teacher at School 10, Mrs. James, asked the class to spell "been" on a quiz.

Flushing, I found I could not write past the letter "b" to begin with, let alone figure whether she wanted a feed bin or a has been. Here, a few days into the year I was washed up. There was so much to learn about how they do things in public school.

One of the smart girls, Cindy, asked if I had gone to a parochial school before moving to Belleville. I said, "No, it was a Catholic school over in Nutley."

The area around School 10 was called Bellwood. Depending on which sage you believed, that stood for Belleville's Woods. Others called it Soho because of the isolation hospital across the street.

The Bellwood Crier interviewed me because I was a new kid in school. The school paper had news, profiles and jokes. I always read the jokes. All I remember from what they printed in their interview of me was that I said I liked the Three Stooges. Alas, if only Mom hadn't cleaned my room in 1966, a few other details about life in those days could be ascertained in a fragile, yellowed copy.

There were three other new kids in class that year. All boys.

Neil's dad had flown racing pigeons back in the Bronx, but he had given them up to move to their new house on Fairway.

Vinnie lived right on Belleville Avenue in a modern-looking house. In sixth grade he had a birthday party there and invited all the boys and girls in our class. Girding nervous grins and sweaty palms, we danced like Clank the Robot in the basement of his split-level house.

Ernie lived over on Fairway somewhere. He had an older sister who didn't go to our school. Sometimes he walked down Carpenter with my classmates. Then, when he got near the apartments on the terrace he cut through the parking lot and private yards as if he owned them.

Ernie was a foot or so taller than me. He palled around with Bobby and Donnie. Bobby lived in the apartments. Donnie lived all the way at the end of Carpenter. He had the longest walk of all of us on the street.

Moe and Hoss, as they later started calling each other were best friends. Once a week they had a knock-down drag-out fight with each other. The next day, always, they were friends again.

Two boys can always get along, but a third usually means something's going to get out of kilter. And so it was that day in the half of the block of Carpenter Street before the apartments that Ernie and I walked. A bunch of rough hooligans, our new classmates, in other words, succeeded in instigating a fracas between the two new kids in class.

Of course, our friends didn't have anything to lose. They didn't have to choose sides. Heck, they hardly knew either one of us very well. They wanted to see the new kids duke it out. What the heck? And most of their money was on the big kid who would whup the little fat kid in no time flat. Who knows, maybe he'd even rip that stupid paisley shirt or make the fat kid's nose bleed.

It didn't take much, whether words or actions, or lies yelled across the sidewalk, that set the 10-year-olds to pushing and shoving. Each, shoving, pushing, talking loud, yet subtly trying to get to the point in the path where the big guy would have to cut away to get home and the other one could walk the rest of the way home with encouraging talk from his neighbors.

With all the rousing from the sidelines, there wasn't much of a fight after all. The big kid swung a roundhouse and missed. The little fat kid used his new leather shoes and with all his might kicked the big kid in the shins.

While the big kid was moaning and groaning, the little fat kid ran off with his buddies. It was over.

No future sportswriter called in the results of the big fight to the Bellwood Crier. In fact, once it was over, nobody ever mentioned it again. Till now, of course.

"Into the WayBack machine, Sherman!"

In sixth grade, Miss Beneziano chose Vinnie and me to work the audio/visual. We got to get out of class and hang out in the auditorium showing science and history films for the other classes. When the films broke down in the projector, between the two of us, we could usually get it rolling again. We also got to work the spotlights for the little kids' plays.

When we were in class, Miss B. had a group of us sit in the front at a separate worktable and she taught us the New Math. She tried, anyway. All I ever got out of the New Math was extra homework that the other kids who sat at their own desks coloring didn't have to do. Therein lay the reward for being smart.

In sixth grade at School 10 I had my first joke published. It was, of course, in the Bellwood Crier.

The first guy says, "Science says that fish is brain food." And the second guy says, "I've been eating it all my life." And the first guy says, "Another scientific theory disproved."

Miss B. got the joke, but I had to explain it to my classmates. I have no idea where I came up with that joke. It was probably on some subversive show beamed in over the airwaves to our old Motorola.

When the next issue of the Bellwood Crier came out, I saw that I had been listed as the editor. Now, I don't remember doing anything special for that newspaper to be named as its editor. I can only guess what inspired Miss B. to list me on the masthead.

Perhaps Miss Beneziano visited a fortune-teller somewhere back there in those pre-hippie days of the not quite late '60s.

"I see, in the crystal ball," the soothsayer said, "in three decades, give or take a couple of years, that funny-looking little blond kid will remember you and this sixth grade class with ink stains that have dried upon some page. Or is that Glenn Campbell I see? No, it's the little boy who shows the movies and shines the spotlight. Glenn Campbell is much taller.

"I also see others of those little boys... one will be on the board of education... another could have been something called Bruce Springsteen but I see him cutting hair - and making a very good living at it too! Yes, some will be doctors and lawyers. And some, those ruffians will be dead or in jail."

So, Miss B., who got married and left school some time after we went on to the junior high, must have taken the prognosticator's words to heart. She named me editor of the Bellwood Crier whether or not I could spell bin for Mrs. James. And ever since, I've been writing about what has been.

Summer peaches in the Rambler

Sucking on a peach pit is the perfect way to while away a steamy summer afternoon.

Roll it around carefully and use the pointed end of the pit to pick out the strands of peach fuzz and pulp between teeth.

All this while the taste of fresh peach tingles through your cheeks.

One of the first things Dad did when we moved into the big house in Belleville was to chop down the black walnut trees and plant a half-dozen peach trees in their stead.

It wasn't long before the low growing peach trees bore fruit and we filled baskets while we decided what to do with the bounty.

Surrounding the small grove of peach trees was Dad's tomato garden. It was about 12 feet across and formed a U about 90 feet long.

Late in spring, he handed me the pitchfork and showed me how to break up the soil in small six- to eight -inch clumps, then turn it over and break it up or down, as the case may be.

He told me I could keep some of the worms for fishing, if I wanted to.

But, of course, being almost a teenager, I knew I could pull up bigger clumps of soil and get the work done much faster and then be off to the fishing hole so much sooner.

This proved that my old man knew what he was talking about when he showed me to work in short narrow lines to turn over the soil.

A few strokes of hauling gargantuan clumps of dirt and turning it over, my way, soon proved to be much too strenuous despite the hurried efforts of a 12-year-old.

Dad started the tomato plants in the small hot house he built next to the garage. When the soil was turned, no mean feat, really, and the green tomato plants large enough, he planted them neatly in the weed-free garden. As the plants grew, Dad attended each stalk and gently tied it off to a homemade stake so it could grow tall and the tomatoes could grow off the ground and away from the bugs and fish bait.

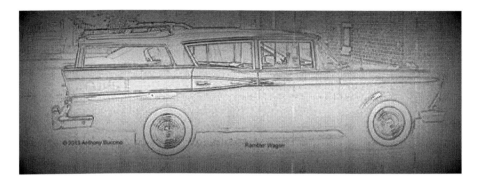

On steamy summer evenings, Dad and I shared the watering duties.

We ran four lengths of 50-foot garden hoses across the length of the yard and let the water run through the dirt paths between the plants.

In the water shortage years, Dad placed five 50-gallon drums at the back of the garage to catch the run-off.

Watering the plants involved a gazillion trips across the yard with a watering pail or two. Watering the garden was a chore best completed before sunset.

After sunset, the Jersey mosquitoes appeared in starving squadrons searching ravenously for the warm-blooded.

Dad did all he could to encourage robins to build nests in the peach, apple and plum trees, but there were never enough bug-eating birds to control the neighborhood flights of blood-sucking mosquitoes.

At first, small green things the size of peas appeared on the tomato vines, and then they grew to the size of cherries.

Almost before our very eyes as the summer waned, there would be big green things about the size of softballs growing on the vines straining the string that held the tall plants to the long thin sticks. Nearly overnight, it always seemed, the tomatoes turned red. Soon there were bushels and bushels of tomatoes.

Mom fixed tomato salads and Dad sent me off with my little red wagon and bags of tomatoes for all the people in the neighborhood.

And we still had "more tomatoes than Carter has pills," Mom used to say.

The peach trees had good years and bad years. Sucking on a peach pit after all these years conjures the good years as clearly as a Norman Rockwell painting. Summer afternoons were spent rolling around with our mutt lying on the grass staring at the perfect tufts of clouds that drifted lazily toward the city.

The big treat of those long ago summers was our annual trip to Olympic Park. That great big amusement park was so far away, we took the Parkway to get there.

Another big summer treat was when Uncle Butch loaded us in Dad's Rambler and took us all the way to Keansburg for a Sunday night at the shore. We spent an evening at the boardwalk, playing games of chance, trying to win some stuff beast or a great big prize. Other times we'd just ride whatever rides appealed to us. Somewhere in the night beyond the dune the ocean waves lapped the shore. But we never swam, never even thought of it, in those days.

The full moon set over the Parkway as we inched our way north. We sat through unbearable traffic. We tried to watch the show at the drive-in theater on Route 35 near Perth Amboy.

We sat as the headlights lit up our car like it was daylight. In the traffic and the fumes, there we were, a tired bunch of kids sprawled behind the back seat, eating peaches from Angelo's trees.

Billy Newtner's bus rides

"BUS NINE RULES!" The older kids shouted. Other kids looked out windows. Girls studied and checked their homework papers. Tough guys with big hands, hard knuckles and big mouths to match, ruled bus nine. They yelled in our fresh faces, "N-O! FUTT NO!"

Many of us seventh graders were hopelessly intimidated by those rough ninth graders and their eighth grade sycophants who ruled our free bus. At the bus stop in winter, they lit cigarettes and said they needed to smoke to keep warm. They ruled the back of the bus. When we were lucky, we got to sit in front next to a friend or near the window with a girl on the aisle. The bullies hardly ever bothered a girl merely to scare the heck out of a seventh grade boy.

The bullies ripped down advertisements from slots over the seats. When they got off the bus, as girls were climbing off, the boys ripped ad signs from the curb side of the bus.

"Where's your weak spot?" They shouted at the toughest of seventh grade boys.

"Where's your weak spot?" He bravely called back across a sea of seated girls.

Sneering in his face, "Be in the gym, seventh period, I'll show you my weak spot!" And they laughed. They laughed at our blank faces which did not understand their jibes. They laughed at the world. They ruled the bus. Around school, they were unnoticed.

Teen Angel, one of our toughest seventh graders, moved to sit among them in the back of the bus. They stuck him in the leg with a safety pin. He bled a bit and laughed it off as sort of an initiation. His auntie complained to the school about him getting a blood clot. Yet, another day's morning announcements ended, "ALL THE BOYS FROM BUS NINE TO THE OFFICE. RIGHT NOW."

Our vice principal, Mr. D, wanted the guilty to confess. "Who ripped off the signs! Those people pay the bus company so you can ride for nothing!

Who's made the young student bleed! A blood clot is a serious thing. A young man could die." And blah, blah, blah.

We younger boys knew it would be the end of us to point a finger. The older boys smirked behind cupped hands. They sneezed 'ah shee--tt' each time the VP looked away. When no one came forward, all boys were banned from the bus for a week.

We reverted to Public Service Bus No. 37, and used our discount tickets. The girls were able to take the free bus from down the corner, we had to walk to Joralemon Street and Franklin Avenue and catch the early pay-bus that made its stops winding all through town. That was the way it had been before the town added our free-bus route.

In 1966, we anticipated the new school, the Junior High, where, as our sixth grade teacher told us, "The teachers there won't treat you like little children. No one is going to chase you for your work. They will give you assignments far ahead, and you will have to be responsible for yourself."

We weren't little babies when we got to Belleville Junior High. We aced orientation day in August. We were smart seventh graders, we knew there was no elevator, and we shouldn't buy elevator tickets from the older kids. We knew which stairwells were up and which were down. We heard the bells to change classes and gym warning bell to get changed.

We knew why the back door of the boys' room was sealed. The vice principal said he tried to catch some boys smoking in there. After they ran out the back door to the cafeteria, he had the door sealed shut.

We knew there was a swimming pool somewhere in the building, but we'd probably never get to see it in our lifetime.

As worldly as we thought ourselves, we were prone to having our books stolen, our pens swiped when we drank at a water fountain, and simply being shoved out of the way by bigger kids going to classes.

Each day, for the first few months we carried to school the excitement of being somewhere new. We were eager to learn in each different class with a different teacher and classes of kids we didn't know who were from other elementary schools.

When we were allowed back on Bus Nine, the boys were subdued for a while. From then on, they called Teen Angel 'Blood Clot'.

"Here comes Blood Clot."

"Blood Clot's gonna' wait for the bus."

"Don't get too close to Blood Clot."

"Who's going to sit next to Blood Clot!"

Each morning the older boys looked out the windows while they teased, taunted and intimidated. They watched for the bus to turn left onto Van Houten Place for the home stretch to High Street behind the school.

Eastbound, Van Houten is wide and slopes downward at about 45-degrees. It intersects with High Street where High has a sharp hill about the same size but going away from Van Houten. When our bus eases into the left turn, the older boys scream "WHOA!" and fall to the right side of the bus falling over one another exaggerating the turn to tip us over.

Whenever a bus driver new to our route would ask us for what street to take everyone shouted different directions. When he turned one way, one group cheered, another groaned. When he turned another way, another group cheered, one group groaned. We led him through Rutan Estates where Plenge's Farm had given way to homes where the kids did not have free buses, but had to walk up to Franklin Avenue and Joralemon St. to catch the 37. ("Where does the 37 bus stop?" the freshman asked us. "About here!") We directed our hopelessly lost bus driver past Nutley schools and a catholic school. Eventually, some girl, who wanted to get in on time to study for a test or get extra help from a teacher, would come forward and direct him to our school. Still, we'd walk in twenty or thirty minutes late and catch the end of homeroom.

After one township tour, I walked into my seventh grade homeroom, late. The teacher yelled, "To the office! You're late! Get out!"

Back out, I went, up the hall and around to the only office I knew. I stood around a few minutes until a guidance counselor asked me what I wanted. "The bus got lost."

"And. . ." she said.

"And. . . I was late for homeroom, Room 104. The teacher said to go to the office," I said.

"Well, who's your teacher?"

I thought for a while. "I don't remember her name. But it's Room 104. It's a science room, with the black top desks that two kids sit at."

Blankly, she stared. Then she said, "Go to your homeroom, I'll straighten it out."

When I got back to homeroom, the teacher wanted to see my pass. "The lady in the office didn't give me one," I said.

My homeroom teacher, who could at once look very pretty and snarly-mean, glared at me as if I was in trouble. "What lady?"

"The lady in the office."

"What office did you go to?" She was mad at me for something.

"The place where you get your classes."

"Sit down."

At that time of the morning, we later learned, teachers either had homerooms or school bus duty.

Each bus had a bus teacher. Ours made sure we all got on the bus safely at night and arrived in tact in the morning. One night I got on the bus where my bus teacher was talking to the driver. I saw that he had put our sign upside-down in the window. I fixed it from the six to the nine. That way, all my friends would get on the right bus where our bus teacher was.

After everybody boarded, we headed home. Our bus driver wouldn't listen to our directions. First he took us to Mill Street, where none of us lived. Then he took us to Silver Lake, where none of us lived and was even farther than the first place he tried to drop us off. We all refused to get off. He told us he couldn't deviate from the route he was given. He had to follow the route for Bus Six. We'd all have to get off.

We told him it was Bus Nine, but he would have none of it. When we still refused to get off the bus, he warned us that he would take us back to the bus terminal. We pleaded that we only wanted to go home, but none of us lived here or back at the first stop. He drove off, but instead of heading toward Celia Terrace or Fairway and Continental avenues, he headed toward Branch Brook Park. He drove us through the park. We protested. We chanted. Nothing worked. Finally, we sat back resigned to being kidnapped by a crazed school bus driver.

Our bus emerged from the park, then crossed Bloomfield Avenue. The driver pulled our bus into huge dark, greasy bus garage and told us all to get out. We still refused. "Then stay there until tomorrow!" He left us there on the bus.

It seemed like we were on that bus for hours. We waited. We waited. Then, we waited some more. Perhaps we would have celebrated New Year's 1968, if he left us there. Ultimately, he came out and drove us back to Belleville. We were so happy to be close to home that we didn't even squawk that he dropped us a few blocks from our real stop. We double-timed home from there.

What befuddled the older boys was that eventually when trouble occurred on the bus, just the boys who caused it were called down. After their punishment, a week or two off the bus, they got on the bus and in our young, stupid faces screeched, "WHO'S THE SQUEALER? SQUEAL, SQUEALER, SQUEAL!"

No one came forward. We may have cringed in fright, but no one came forward. I was in the alcove to the VP's office one morning when one of the good older kids came out from the VP's office. Shortly afterward he called down the few bullies who had acted up earlier. This kid was tall and lanky, but not one of the bullies.

"A cowardly squealer," I thought. How could he turn in these bullies who wreck the bus and scare the daylights out of us younger kids. My sympathy for the bullies was brief. This nerdy ninth grader was a good spy, like James Bond. Here was a meek bookworm taking on heroic proportions at great personal risk.   The bullies from Bus Nine certainly would have beaten him and his weak spot to a pulp if they knew it was him who now turned them in at every ill deed. I told Teen Angel who the squealer was, but he didn't believe me, and we never told anyone else.

The following year, the ninth graders had moved up to the high school, and the rowdy eighth graders had gone off to catholic high school where they were taught by all-men who believed in corporal punishment and gave number grades instead of letter grades.

In 1969, we became top dogs on the bus. There were no bigger guys to boss us around, so we fought among one another. The same kids who were bullies in fifth and sixth grade continued through ninth grade. Our tough guys would sneak their friends on our bus. They'd have "mock-out" fights insulting each other and their mothers. The kids who went on to the next stop invariably hurled insults from the windows as they were driven away. And one of our tough sneak-ons, showing off as usual, kicked the side of the bus as it pulled away.

The next day came the familiar refrain. . . "ALL THE BOYS FROM BUS NINE TO THE OFFICE. RIGHT NOW."

We were probably toughest on new kids, seventh graders without bigger brothers who would kick our butts. Our second stop in the morning and first stop after school was on Celia Terrace. We knew some of the boys there from our ice hockey matches at Fairway Park.

Little Billy Newtner, our tough guys called him, was in our grade but not in any of our classes. He got on at the second stop, so none of our crowd knew whether he lived in a house or the garden apartments. He was smaller and shorter than the rest of us and had short curly hair. We called him Billy Newtner, but none of us knew his real name. It was just that he was different and spoke through his nose somehow and that was how his name sounded to the tough guys.

Seeing him get on the bus, the tough guys held their noses and shouted, "Hey-yo, Biwwee Newtner! Haw wa you tanay? Biwwee Newtner!"

He always smiled when they first said his name. He seemed to be happy to be recognized by his friends on Bus Nine. He withdrew his perfect teeth and sucked in his smile, as he realized they were making fun of his voice. He stared straight ahead and sat in the first open seat.

"You haww a giw fwen, Biwwee Newtner?"

"You gaw a da-et faw da dan Sayer nay, Biwwee Newtner?"

Taunting continued until his eyes were red, or the bus arrived at school. It was not often Billy Newtner rode the bus home, but no one noticed or missed him.

One day two short-skirted girls rode our bus home. Their miniskirts exposed the longest legs in the world. In school skirt hems were supposed to be at knee top, but that didn't sway these girls. They were fourteen going on twenty. They swapped insults with each other like no girls we had ever seen. They mocked each other's hair color, style and falls, fake long hair that somehow stayed in. When they finally got off at Continental they were so mad at each other they started fighting. Boys from our stop drew together in a circle around the girls. They slapped and pushed and ripped at each other's clothes. They pulled each other's hair. Their short skirts rose and boys glimpsed their underwear. They rolled on someone's lawn and the boys got another eyeful. When they tired of battering each other they walked away with torn stockings and broken belt loops but otherwise uninjured.

A fat-faced girl got on our bus at Celia each morning. She never said two words to anyone, least of all to our tough guys. Yet they mocked this fat girl, they mocked her glasses, and they shouted her down when she dared answer them. They said she looked like a Russian farm girl. They called her many names but the one that stuck was "Kamikaze Communist Girl" which was usually followed by "Zigg - Kyle!" and a salute. Other than the Celia Terrace kids, none of us ever knew her by anything other than "Kamikaze Communist Girl".

No heroes came forward to rat out these bullies. No heroics on Bus Nine, from grade nine or anywhere.

Yellow cracker school days

That distinctive smell of pizza and french fries on Friday mornings always signaled the school week was nearly over.

A few minutes in the lunch line, and one or two classes, and it's onto the weekend.

Not only the children felt this way, but some adults went to four years and more of college, got certified and are allowed to cram an adult meal into their gullets in 20 minutes or less.

Now, that's dedication.

As one who brown-bagged it 99 percent of the time, I often pitied the bus kids who had to buy the hot lunch in the school cafeteria. Theirs was an endless stream of mystery meat in brown gravy with vegetables no one could identify.

Plus Jell-O, of course.

Surely, at that price, it was a bargain, but what it was was anybody's guess.

Luckily for me, Mom packed the sandwich – wrapped in Cut-Rite waxed paper – an orange – scored, of course or an apple or a pear, and a pack of Funny Bones or a Ring Ding.

Sandwiches were predictable, made from the best cold cuts in the world, ham, turkey or bologna and cheese, usually on white bread.

Sometimes there would be a meatball sandwich on Italian bread.

Or on special occasions, Mom set aside a veal cutlet or two from dinner and I had that for lunch, much to the drooling envy of my table mates.

However, to wash it all down, I was at the mercy of the lady who sold the milk at the milk island.

If I got there early enough, there'd be at least one half-pint of chocolate milk.

In junior high, they sold tumblers of fresh orange juice for almost nothing, but you had to go through the main cafeteria line with everybody else to buy it.

After lunch and before the bell rang, a classmate got a tray of the tumbler-sized glasses of cold, wet orange juice and drank them down one after another as if they were iced beers on a hot summer afternoon.

They all went down so easily.

School cafeterias always had the greatest food accessories.

My favorite cafeteria snacks were the yellow crackers with the peanut butter filling. In the old days, a school cafeteria was the only place you could buy those six-pack crackers.

For variety, they had orange crackers with yellow filling. These treats were held together with preservatives and red dye number three.

Only in the school cafeteria could we find the three-pack of chocolate chip or oatmeal cookies.

These cookies, although packaged, were soft and chewy – before it became a marketing ploy – and had a fresh-baked taste as in the days when Mom baked cookies and Dad went to work.

If you were quick enough and got into the cafeteria line early, you could grab a piece of blueberry pie.

Sometimes after I finished what Mom packed, I'd check to see if they put out the pie for the next lunch class.

There was something addictive about my school cafeteria blueberry pie.

In a pinch, it could pass for a whole meal, but it served as dessert, too.

Kids who ate the hot meals raved about the broiled potatoes.

These crispy brown wonders were charred with a secret spice combination of olive oil and oregano that was brushed on by women with their hair in buns.

On Fridays, the covert operation was to distract a table mate while an accomplice swiped a french fry or two.

This was always good for a knowing laugh.

Cafeterias were built to provide an outlet for the kids' mid-day hyper energy.

Usually the walls were tiled to give the proper echo to the din. Kids often left the cafeteria and went straight to the nurse's office for Q-tips. Conversations were raucous shouts.

Directions from teachers who could not weasel out of cafeteria duty were lost in the lion's roar.

It was useless to tell the cafeteria lady, "No veggies," because she could not hear you and gave them to you anyway.

A student shut in at an elementary lunch reported that they were not allowed to talk at lunch.

Perhaps the armed matron watching over the youngsters was born with a perpetual headache and children bothered her.

But a kid who talked in that lunch ended the day serving time in elementary school detention hell.

Nowadays, the cafeteria ladies, God bless 'em, are said to listen to rock 'n' roll music on WKTU.

If they ever had a radio in the old days, it would have been tuned to the all-polka AM station.

Radios in those days could not pick up the signal in the old stone buildings.

When we were in school, we never had a chance to reminisce about the TV shows we watched when we were little.

If anything, we talked about last night's "Fugitive" or the "Mod Squad."

"Sesame Street" didn't start until I was in high school.

The kids today stumble into a friendly game of "remember when" every now and then.

You can hear the rumble, "Thunder! Thunder! Thunder Cats!"

Then they break away into their sentimental memories of Rainbow Brite.

And so it is when I see an ice cream sandwich. It has been more than 25 years since I queued up with my hearty youthful appetite for those yellow peanut butter cookies and an ice cream sandwich to wash them down.

For a brief moment or two, I long to be in junior high school again.

Maybe I should have been a teacher.

Or maybe a quick visit to a real school cafeteria with living, breathing brats in their oversize clothes with their indecipherable jive will quash this longing.

Selling pretzels at school football games

As the Indian summer bids a hasty retreat, eventide arrives sooner and sooner, the novelty of the new school year quickly wanes.

The fall fashions have already made their flash in the school hallways, children wonder will this outfit be too warm for school or that outfit too cool?

This is the time of the school year when the older kids look forward to the big game on Saturday.

Nowadays, families struggle to be everywhere for each child's Saturday games. That is why there is so much talk about cloning. First we start with sheep, then cattle, then mom and dad. It's the only way to be everywhere at the same time.

In simpler times, like when I was in high school, there was only one game in town on autumn afternoons. First, we'd shoo the terrible terra-dactyls and dactylettes, then the field would be ours.

The big kids of the senior class and selected junior varsity guys would take to the field and roll around on the grass trying to do gym class routines in padding and uniforms so tight, we wondered how they could move at all, let alone play football. In the course of inter-school athletics, both teams had to wear the same restrictive uniforms to keep it all even.

For some of the younger players, this pre-game exercise was the only chance they would have to take the field, let alone get any dirt on their clean bright uniforms.

It was not simply for the sport of play on the field that we gathered. For the high school kids, this Saturday football game was as much a part of social life as any debutante ball or junior promenade.

On autumn Saturdays through those treacherous teen years the different age groups would appear at the high school game for sundry reasons. Most pre-teens actually went to watch the game and root, root, root for the home team.

The pubescents sought out their own, and like strange dogs meeting for the first time, they spied, sniffed and checked each other pubescent and gathered under the Saturday sun.

My best friend Teen Angel worked at a local bakery-deli for a few years. His uncle Harry pushed and pulled and got him in with Ed Strat at Belle Maid on Joralemon Street near the Rec House in Belleville.

In our junior year Teen Angel asked me if I wanted to make some money. At a time when it cost five bucks to fill the old VW Bug, a little cash came in handy. Teen Angel's boss needed young men with weak minds and strong backs to hustle his wares at the Saturday football games.

It was a terrific job. I got to wear a harness that held the pretzel basket and a carpenter's apron for my money and change.

They sent me out from under the concrete bleachers into the crowds and I yelled, "Pretzels! Pretzels!" and people would call me up the rows and rows of bleachers to buy a pretzel or two.

As first jobs go, there were lumps that tagged along.

There were always some smart aleck kids who timed it just right so that when you turned away, they could pelt you with a chunk of pretzel from your blind side. There was never any way to know who threw it. Such was the yoke of working in the real world.

And, of course, every sleazy classmate I spent my academic career avoiding suddenly professed undying friendship – now, if only I could sneak them a few free pretzels, my boss wouldn't mind. After all, what are good friends for?

These guys would have been the first to clobber me with a chunk of pretzel.

When the game was over, Teen Angel and I headed back to the bakery-deli where he would work a while. I would wait around to get paid.

In the meantime he showed me around the empty back room. That's where the bakers used the giant mixing bowls to make the dough to make the donuts. Teen Angel didn't work in the kitchen, only at the counter, but he showed me what they used to make the crumb topping on coffee cake and crumb buns. It was a trade secret, more or less.

And I waited to get paid.

It wasn't much of a pay, but it covered an LP or two. And at other times it filled the tank for my friends and me to make merry in those puerile days.

But after a season, I turned in my carpenter's apron and the basket harness and left the concrete bleacher steps to others with weak minds and strong backs.

By my senior year I was much too sophisticated to hawk pretzels. It was all about image in the bleachers. I called the kid to come up a few rows. I bought a pretzel or two, for old time's sake.

Job rock in prose

In 1970 my 11th grade English class at Belleville High School was broken down into several groups to do a group book report. The group I was in selected **The Strawberry Statement Notes of a College Revolutionary** by James Simon Kunen.

Of the five students in my group, I was the only one who read the book through in three days and started reading it again. No one else in my group even liked the book and struggled to read it at least once.

I loved that book. It became a second bible to me. I began writing after reading that book, and most of my early writings were in that off-beat unrelated style. It was fun being a writer. I'd tell anyone who asked, "Yeah, I'm writing a book." They'd always ask, "About what?" I'd usually mumble, "You'll have to see when it comes out," trailing off, then avoiding that person for a week or more.

One of my favorite writers, Bob Dylan, was once asked what he wanted to be, he told the interviewer, "a movie usher." That's great. It says a lot of people have other things in mind to be doing other than what they are doing. Here are some of mine:

I've been a shoe salesman, and let me tell you, t was no fun. It used to take me fifty minutes in the back room each time I had to find a pair of ladies' pumps. I lost the job when the boss didn't like the way I'd refiled the shoes. I thought it would be easier if two left shoes of different sizes were in every box. That way, I figured, the lady would have an option to match her foot size. After I'd rearranged the whole back room with my unique filing system, he let me go. He fired me, just like that.

Before the oil embargo I wanted to be a gas station attendant, washing windows, checking oil, pumping gas, etc. The highlight of that career would have been explaining mechanical malfunctions. I'd do it this way: "Sorry ma'm, your gravistan is jammed in the forkistran. What we need to fix it is a monolithic jack fork lift to separate and recoil the semi-conductor rectifier. It'll take two weeks and cost about eighty-five thousand dollars." I figure a couple of big jobs like that and I could retire.

Another of my occupational fantasies is to be an over-the-road truck driver. I'd wheel my big rig over the interstate highways talking in code over the CB radio about "smokies" down the road. The best job I could get in this line of work would be as a roadie for a pop star hauling equipment from New York to Detroit in three hours.

Related to the 'roadie' image, another over-the-road job would be as a security guard in a private, marked patrol car. I'd have a siren and impressive strobe lights on top of the car. The facet of this occupation that excites me most is the dashboard cluttered with gadgets that would summon assistance if an emergency should arise.

An occupation that would satisfy my thirst for law enforcement is the walking, chalking, work-a-day life of a meter maid. Of course, I couldn't be a meter maid. I don't look so good in skirts, I learned that when my sister dressed me funny. But I'd still like to be a ticket writer-outer on the avenue. You'd never see a man as happy as me when I've nailed a double parked car at a yellow curb. The mere thought of this thrill makes my fingers twitch nervously for a pen and a ticket book.

There's still another occupation where I could work with parked cars and never have to chalk a tire or do any writing. I'd stand outside Lipton's back door collecting money (fifty cents) and give people pieces of paper for validation and refund. I could really go for that job. Even if I had to bring out the "Lot Full" sign, it's worth it just to wear the change maker on my belt.

It boils down to only one other line of work for which I'd settle. It would unite me with "man's best friend." I'd like to be the dog walker for Lenore's Canine Clippery in Belleville. All I'd need to work there is a borrowed leash, a shovel, and a broom. While the little rascals are waiting for a wash and trim, I would take them for a promenade around the block. Or after they've been primped, out we'd go: man and his best friend, side by side.

Back in high school, I had a friend who wanted to be a garbage man because "they only work two days a week." Let me close by saying, "It isn't all that meets the eye."

Peter Pan Revisited, again

It's been a long time since I've thought much about Peter Pan, much less my freshman English class production of the rock 'n' roll version called affectionately "Peter Pan Revisited."

It's been nearly 25 years since I cast off the coils of high school and almost 30 years since that first play, but many memories of those rehearsals and those freshman classmates appear before me and the stage is set every time I close my eyes.

September of 1968 started out mostly like any other school year. The mornings were cool enough to need a jacket and the hot afternoons left us longing to shuck our clothes and jump in every swimming pool all along the way home.

In English that year we would not have to diagram sentences. That's what our new teacher, Bob Leffelbine, told us. We were going to learn about literature, and of course there would be vocabulary. It wasn't just spelling anymore. After all, we were freshmen and this was supposed to be our prelude to high school and the real world.

However, it was not long before that English teacher started talking to us about stage left, stage right and the other parts of the stage. He was excited telling us about the stage and asides and soliloquies and other terms of the theater.

It was all new to us, but his enthusiasm somehow sank into the freshman minds and before we knew it we had become as enthralled as he was with this stage stuff and, yes, acting too.

Amidst his explanation of the parts of the play and the roles of the actors, in walked the lady who was the head of the English department.

'Leff' quickly bridged to a diatribe on mythology and Greek gods and Roman gods. We stared, entranced by this sudden new material and strange names as he droned on about Zeus, Ares, Janus, Jason and the Argonauts.

We thought he would never run out of exposition about the legends and myths. To us mostly 14-year-olds, our English teacher seemed to be about a 100, even though he dressed like some of our older brothers.

And his lesson abruptly ended when his department chair left the class. He switched back to the place where his love proved to be, in the production of a play, and without asking us. Somehow he knew that we would be the cast and crew of his production. We were sure that whatever he came up with, we who were without any training in theater would do justice to the show.

This crew of neo-thespians he had acquired by luck of the English classes he drew to teach soon pitched in to, as Judy Garland and Mickey Rooney used to say in those corny old movies, "Let's put on a show!"

Not only were we suddenly dedicated to the production of a silly little play he wrote called, "Peter Pan Revisited," but we were so excited that many of us came in to rehearse our parts during the Christmas vacation week.

It was a sure bet that none of these kids would have come into school during a vacation for any other reason at any other time.

But there was something in the way this whole play-thing was presented that our English teacher sparked an untapped desire in us, even the ones of us who would never step on a stage again for the rest of their lives.

We all were drawn in to the excitement. Even those among us who didn't care about the play, who would never sing on the stage, whose only job was to move a piece of scenery or stand behind Peter when Captain Hook and the bad guys came along.

All of us non-essential actors realized that as long as we were working on this silly little play, then we would not have to learn anything in English class.

So, watching the other kids work on the stage, watching them learn about blocking, upstage and down stage, and voice projection and ultimately how to lip-sing to their own tapes, was for the rest of us all a break from actually learning anything, we reasoned.

What could be better than going through a whole school year and not having to learn anything?

Of course, there were a few moments when the supporting cast got out of hand. While the leading cast was singing on-stage, some of us, and I won't say who, had other things going on.

One of the more creative among us took the copy of the script he had and reworked all the dialogue into the foulest language any of us knew. It was shocking and hysterically funny at the same time. Who could expect 14-year-old boys to be serious forever and not somehow bring sex into everything they do? Fortunately, our English teacher/director/playwright never knew what those boys in the back of the auditorium were laughing at.

Our teacher had a play to produce, and, by God, the show must go on.

As we got closer to the performance dates of our version of "Peter Pan Revisited" we found that his other English classes had been enlisted to work on scenery and put our class of actors into make-up.

The other class showed up with fishing tackle boxes of poufy creams and tubes of goo that they insisted on putting not only on our faces but on the back of our hands as well as any part of our flesh that would otherwise give us a ghostly hue as we were washed out in the high-intensity lights beaming on each of us from the proscenium.

This fossilized English teacher of ours was not using kiddy make-up on us. He was using the real stuff just like they use on real stage actors. And this real-professional style make-up stuff only came off with real actor-type deep-cleaning cleanser that made your face and even the back of your hands sting as you removed the make-up goo. Mary Ann Castellano put on my makeup. I was one of Peter's guys and I had to wear green. I didn't have any lines, and I stood behind a rock.

Before we actually took the stage, 'Leff' told us about stage lore, such as "It's bad luck to whistle in a dressing room," and never say, "good luck" to an actor.

And believe it or not, want it or not, when the stage was set and the lights were lit, and that curtain went up, we were all actors who gave our all to the show that our English teacher wrote and called "Peter Pan Revisited."

So in all these nearly 30 years since that play helped me squeak through another year of high school English without learning anything, or so I thought at the time, I've learned a few things about that old English teacher.

First of all, he wasn't really as old as Methuselah. As a matter of fact, most 14-year-olds don't have a whole lot of perception between being 25 and 55, so old is old.

In fact, the year we had him and he put us into that silly little play he wrote called "Peter Pan Revisited" was his first year as an English teacher. And at the time the writing and production and success of it was no less an achievement than Charles Dickens scribbling "Great Expectations."

Our English teacher was running on enthusiasm and passion. And he past that on to us in the year we had together. But ours wasn't the only class that benefited from his passion for performance.

Through these nearly 30 years, other classes have come and gone and, I'm sure, earned their respect of my freshman class English teacher through whatever capacity he used to touch their hearts.

In the years since he taught my class and kept his heart in acting and theater we had occasion to talk a time or two. And he always had a bright smile and a great big, read: sincere, hello.

So, the last time I saw him he was in a teachers' talent show to benefit something or another. Ironically he had no lines, he simply stood down stage as a director watching the long-legged dancer on the stage.

Perhaps he was Bob Fosse and the dancer Cyd Charisse, or perhaps that is what memory does. But forever I shall remember him as the director.

For all he taught me when I didn't think I was learning, thanks for the memories, Bob.

Back to school, institutional green

One of the best things about Amazon.com is that you can look for out of print titles and if they are available buy them and be reading them in no time.

In the old days, you might have had to go to a used book store and browse the stacks for hours to find a treasure.

(Reminds me of the argument in **The Strawberry Statement, Notes of A College Revolutionary** by James Simon Kunen - where he passes a Hard-To-Find-Records store and argues that if the record is in the store then it can't be too hard to find. But I digress.)

One of those lost treasures I recovered recently was a copy of a book I lost in 1971 or so right in front of my house while I was playing street hockey.

I had laid the book, **Our Time Is Now; Notes From the High School Underground**, edited by John Birmingham, down with my school books and later when I got inside it had gone missing. I can remember a lot of things about that book. One thing was the phrase Institutional Green and Johnny Potseed and the kissy girl with the bad breath on the long bus ride. Institutional green referred to the room paint in the schools. Johnny Potseed was a how-to article and the girl on the bus, I'll get to that shortly.

Of course they were stories, you know, just a lot of words I read almost 40 years ago but they left some sort of impression on me.

Between Kunen's book and Birmningham's collection of writings from the underground student newspapers, oh, and probably the full side of Dylan songs on The Concert for Bangla Desh, in that whirlwind force field I decided to become a writer.

In the old days, before the Internet, when computers were as big as classrooms and programmed in FORTRAN with keypunch cards, the only way to publish alternative information was with a printing press of some kind and lots of paper.

Published in 1970, OUR TIME is a collection of writings from high school student published underground newspapers from the late sixties. The papers had names like SMUFF, LINKS, SANSCULOTTES, T.R.I.P., COMMON SENSE, THE OBSERVED, FREETHINKER, MINSTREL, WEAKLY READER, and, of course, my favorite, INSTITUTIONAL GREEN.

When I finally connected with my replacement copy, I opened the familiar brown cover with its clenched red, white and blue painted fist, and began thumbing through.

Within a ten page spread of the back of the book, on Page 264, I found the passage I remember about INSTITUTIONAL GREEN and the girl with bad breath riding on a bus.

The unsigned story from INSTITUTIONAL GREEN, New York, is titled BATHROOMS, and as well as I remembered it, when I reread it, it all came back to me.

The author was trying to describe the smell of the school bathrooms. Ultimately, the smell takes him back to when he was 12 and rode on a long bus trip. A girl sat in his lap and they started making out.

The girl, it turned out, as you already know, had bad breath. Says the author, "Well, that's what the bathrooms in this school remind me of. Don't tell me I'm a kook, because I'll be sorry I told you."

Students in the underground newspapers then fought for girls to attend boys' schools (Page 139 - GIRL IN STUYVESANT? - Weakly Reader No. 10.)

In ATTENTION ALL TEACHERS! - MINE, No. 8, Tucson, Ariz., the underground newspaper refers to the biology text: "in about one year, you (the students) will have forgotten about 85 percent of the facts you learned in biology and that the purpose of the course was not to have you memorize facts, but to put you in a frame of thinking, in this case scientific."

Larry Siegal writes of JOHNNY POTSEED in SANSCULOTTES No. 30, NY, on Page 246. Just a few pages later Lenny Lubart writes WNEW-FM: A NEW VOICE IS HEARD in THE FORUM, VOL. I, No. 5, Paramus, N.J.

Birmingham, the editor of OUR TIME, began his underground newspaper career at the school newspaper in Hackensack, N.J. He was graduated Hackensack in 1969 and went on to attend New York University.

OUR TIME carries an introduction by Kurt Vonnegut, Jr. How cool is that!

1970 was the year the seniors nailed my English literature book to the shop class table with a 10-penny nail. I needed a crowbar to pry it off the workbench and the hammer to pound the nail back out. We had the world by the balls and none of us knew it.

1970, it was the last time I wanted to be an astronaut. Or a fireman.

Back then the moon was made of green cheese & Pluto was still a planet (was the planet named after the cartoon character, or was the cartoon dog named after the planet? And why does Goofy talk but Pluto doesn't? And what about Belushi's character in Animal House? What was his name?)

In our health class we had to struggle to find ten songs with drug references in them. Lucy in the Sky with Diamonds, was one. Vietnam was a dirty little war and most of the kids in my high school couldn't tell you the name of one kid from our town who had died over there. Neither could I tell you one of them was my cousin.

A few years later, when I was a senior, I got on the student newspaper. We never managed to publish one issue of the student paper.

We did, however, have a page to run stuff in the Belleville Times. Those were my very first bylines. You can look them up if you don't have anything better to do.

But be careful, something you may read just might stick in the back of your head for the next 40 years.

Just another day on Police Beat

It was just another day on Police Beat. I cover Police Beat. That's my job. That's what I do. Walking through cluttered halls, checking out wanted posters, looking for someone I know, someone I could turn in. None of the posterized people look familiar. I'd have to stop counting the reward money. Guess all my friends are dead or in jail or have real jobs.

Like I said in the last paragraph, I cover Police Beat. That's my job. That's what I do. I check out the blotter, call up the cases that interest me. Check 'em out with the cops on duty. Then I come into this newspaper and tell you about them. That's your job. You read all about it. You smack yourself in the head and say, "there but for the grace of God..."

I like Police Beat. Usually I hear about the good stuff before you do. But if you hear about it before me, you always call me to see if I know. You tell me what you want to read. I write it. That's my job. Keep that straight and you'll get along fine on Police Beat.

It was Tuesday. Last week. I was on Police Beat. That's my job. That's what I do. I cruised through the concrete mountain called Belleville Town Hall. Found the stairs, then worked my way down. I looked left, saw the police desk. Nah, they'll have to get along without me this morning. I'm looking for Police Beat. That's my job. That's what I do.

I saw the Coke machine. I knew I was getting close to the detectives. They work nights. They need sugar. They need a Coke machine. It's a friendly Coke machine. Not like those fancy hotel machines. Sure, there's one on every floor, but a buck a can? That's outrageous. When I'm on Hotel Beat, I call room service and pay two bucks plus tip, and charge it to the boss. But that's another story.

I get past the Coke machine with only a minor flashback. Then I'm on my way. I round the corner. The ladies room catches my eye. Another flashback

When I was Investigative Reporter, I went undercover, slipped into the ladies room and took clandestine pictures of the holes in the floor. The cover story issued by the building department was that they were doing some plumbing work. They said they had to put a two foot hole in the floor next to the sink and the mirror so the pipes would have a place to leak.

Another story is that a few female prisoners barricaded themselves in and tried to dig their way out with plastic Sporks that came with their take-out food. That's a story I'll save for a rainy day.

I cover Police Beat. That's my job. That's what I do. I head over to the records window. It's the same window the public visits to see how the police wrote up their accident report. Fifty cents a copy, the good reports go for two bucks. The glass came from a bank that closed down in 1929.

I stick my nose in the window. Usually that's-all it takes for them to know it's me. I cover Police Beat. I have a nose for news. I'm known for my nose. Sticking your nose through the peephole can be dangerous. That's my job. Sometimes it's dangerous.

This is where the brains of the department are. The center of operations. The plug it in and watch the sparks computer. It's all here. On Police Beat. Just one flight down from the first floor and one flight up from the basement.

I say the password here on Police Beat. They let me in. I walk through. I try not to knock any of the catch-all files filed around where I can catch them with my camera bag. I always carry my camera in a camera bag. I may have to be Jimmy Olsen someday, I have to be ready. And, anyway it gives me a place for my Lifesavers. On Police Beat, you never know when you'll need a Lifesaver.

The lieutenant points to my chair. I sit down. We talk. We talk about the weather. One day it's hot. One day it's cold. We're all going to catch pneumonia, we both say. We laugh. You have to laugh on Police Beat. It's not part of the job. But it helps.

I take out a notebook from my camera bag. The floor looks dry next to my chair. I set the camera bag on the floor. Over by the lieutenant's desk he's not so lucky. The tiles have come up. When he pushes down slightly with his foot, water squishes through the cracks. If it weren't so pathetic, we'd laugh.

The lieutenant says that's how he knows when he has to get new shoes. The water comes up through the floor and through his shoes, and that's when he knows when to get new shoes. It almost passes for a joke.

Look at this, he says. The desk came from DeWitt Savings bank when they got new furniture. Look at it now. The lieutenant opens the drawer. It is warped. With his foot he touches a bottom panel on the wooden breakfront. It falls in to a little puddle. This is not a pleasant site on Police Beat.

I've got to get the news, I say to him. That's my job. That's what I do. He fills me in on crime. I count in my head all the cars that are stolen here and end up in Newark. If they're recovered at all.

The lieutenant throws me a curve. A stolen car was recovered in East Orange. We figure they must have taken a wrong turn somewhere. On Police Beat, we don't interpret the news, we report it. That's my job. That's what I do.

I ask about the flowing water under the floor tiles. My News Nose takes over. I've got to know more about it.

The lieutenant says on Monday morning, it's 200 degrees here in his office. He opens the window, but the heat won't leave the room. The only way to stop the heat, he says, is turn off the radiator. When you turn off the radiator, it leaks.

We're here in the basement, and some people may call it hell, but it doesn't have to be that hot, I say, speaking for Police Beat.

The lieutenant nods.

My time is up. I get up to leave Police Beat. I put my notebook in my camera bag. I look at the lieutenant. Here on Police Beat, I've become a victim.

Lookit here, lieutenant, I say. Feel this, lieutenant, I say, handing him my camera bag. It was dry when I came in here, I say. It's soaked now. But I put it down where the tiles are in place, I protested. It's not fair. The floor should only leak where there are no tiles. It shouldn't leak where my camera bag works as a sponge and sucks the water through the cracks in the floor.

The lieutenant looks at me. He looks at my sopping camera bag. Here on Police Beat, the words are unsaid. They don't need to be said. The lieutenant and I both know what must be done.

It's time for Police Beat to get pasted to the pages and call out Editorial Man. Yes, that wordy character from another mindset, who has the power to get leaking fire house roofs fixed, broken doors repaired, and, least of all, doorknobs replaced.

That strange character who will turn up before you know it and put ideas in your head that you'll have thought you've always had. Yes, he's on his way, on his way to investigate the wet floor on Police Beat. From Police Beat, he'll get one tip. Bring your own Lifesavers.

Memories of Brookdale soda

I never drank milk except in coffee when I was a kid. That was back in the days when milkmen made house calls.

In our neighborhood on Gless Avenue in Belleville, New Jersey, we had strong young fellows who delivered our cases of 12-pack Brookdale soda bottles.

The men, strong and sure, gripped the cases, one in each hand and lugged our soda up the stairs to our second floor apartment.

I remember those big strong young men and the quiet summers on a dead end street. It's funny, here, now, so many years later, how this old soda bottle brings me back home...

We drink Brookdale soda in my house. It's the only kind we buy. It says right on every bottle, "Pride of the Garden State."

It satisfies better than the TV-hyped soda and it's the soda pop I grew up with.

When I was a kid, I called the fruit punch flavor 'blood' and the cherry pit flavor tickled and chilled my chest after a hard day of play.

On my first visit to Ashtabula, Ohio, the summer dog day afternoon sun dried me out.

"Soda, please?" I asked my new friends. I waited for them to break out the Brookdale.

My throat was parched. My kingdom for a glass of Brookdale soda, I thought.

In the land of Buckeyes, where they think the Garden State has something to do with Eden, the place, not the TV star, I got a very, very tall glass of club soda!

Yuk! It tasted like the sands of Iwo Jima. What made matters worse was, it wasn't even Brookdale! How foreign can you get?

The people in Ohio, (it really is in the U.S., though you can't prove it by what they drink) call soda "pop."

So, if you're ever out that way and the water doesn't fancy your suit, don't ask, "Soda, please?" Unless you're on a new diet.

I should put in to collect hazard pay for attempting to put ice in my Brookdale soda.

Lately, as my adulthood approaches, I've flavored Kola flavor. It's not cola, or un-cola, it's Kola! And I think it tastes best with lots of ice in a tall glass.

Every time I open the freezer door, a rock hard package of Sara Lee's dessert crashes onto my bare feet.

I won't say I'm a slow learner, but after about the fourth time around, I tried moving back with the freezer door when I opened it for the ice.

Good idea, right? I thought so, but that crumb cake was smarter than that. It waited until I stepped around to get the tray, then it crashed. I put some ice in a glass and the rest on my foot.

If it keeps up like this, the soda made from artesian well water may just be my downfall. Unless, and I just thought of this, unless I put the whole bottle in the freezer, then I won't have to get the ice!

Hmmmm. That sounds like a cool, safe idea for a hot summer night, doesn't it? But I better remember the bottle or I'll really have something to write the folks in Ashtabula about. I just remembered that those sealed bottles tend to explode when they freeze. I grew up with that too, on the back porch, in the cold, cold winter nights in Belleville, New Jersey.

Brown bagging lunch through the years

In my most recent job, I brought in my lunch, too, and ate in in the last hour before my lunch break. That gave me time to do other things, write notes to myself, take photos of the city around me, be it the surprising reflections of Jersey City, or the myriad facets of each turn around Times Square.

On Sunday night I'd make my own sandwiches for the week. I'd spread before me, one sheet of aluminum foil, ten paired slices of bread, the packets of cold cuts, and the squeeze mustard bottle. I'd set to work dividing the sliced turkey and American cheese into five equal mounds on the bread. Then I'd plop a bit of mustard and cover with the second slice of bread.

Then each sandwich was whisked to its own awaiting shining sheet of foil, folded thusly, again and again into a square and set aside. Repeat four more times and load the silver packets into fridge.

When I attended Holy Family School in Nutley and lived down the block on Gless Avenue in Belleville, I'd go home each day where my lunch would be waiting. I'd sit in the living room eating as Mom and I watched her stories, Love of Life, Search for Tomorrow and Guiding Light. That lasted through fourth grade.

In the winter, sometimes, when mom was busy in another room, I'd set my sandwich on the hot radiator and it would crisp or burn a bit on one side. Everyone knew that the toaster was for making toast when you had that for breakfast. Whoever would have thought to toast my Wonder bread for brooklunch?

When we moved from Gless Avenue crosstown to Carpenter Street, school opened but we didn't move into the new house until mid-October. At School Ten, my fifth grade teacher said she was thinking only of me when she suggested I not eat lunch in school, it was so very rare in those days, as I wouldn't then be allowed to play outside until the bell rang us in.

My first day in the new school, our plan was for me to go into Harry's Sweet Shop on Belleville Avenue and there eat the lunch my mom prepared.

Harry was a nice guy, I'm sure, but we soon realized he didn't like the idea of even one kid coming into his counter area to eat a brown bag lunch, and promptly shooed me out his door and into the strange neighborhood to eat.

The next day, Mom met me behind on Arthur Street, a dead end behind the school, and I ate my lunch in the car. When I finished eating, I got out of the car and went to hang around the school playground until it was time to go in.

Mom and I did this for a while, maybe a week, maybe a couple of weeks or so until one of my new classmates, Paul Calabrese, stopped to ask what's up. I was one of four new boys in that fifth grade class, but I was the only one who met his mother on a side street and ate his lunch in a parked car.

Paul asked his mother and they invited me to bring my lunch and eat at their house until we moved in. We became buddies for a while and after school my mom would pick me up at his house. Being on separate sides of busy Belleville Avenue we didn't pal around much after I moved in and made friends with the guys in the neighborhood.

For the rest of my time at School Ten, I ate lunch at home, at my own kitchen table or in the living room, while helping Mom catch up on her stories.

Seventh grade brought us all into the world of taking the 37 Bus or later Bus Nine to Belleville Junior High School. My lunches, as Mom prepared them, were brown bagged, with a scored orange and a packet of Yodels or Funny Bones, and a napkin. I was on my own to secure a chocolate milk to help wash it down.

I never understood how so many kids could buy that hot lunch, with vegetables, no less, or those wrapped sandwiches in cellophane. All I ever bought at the school cafeteria were those peanut butter crackers that came six to a pack, chocolate milk or orange juice, and then I washed that and my homemade brown bag lunch down with an ice cream sandwich.

My taste in cold cuts was rather pedestrian, running the brief gamut of boiled ham, salami, bologna, and cheese, and then back again.

Sometimes I'd open my plain brown bag to find a sandwich filled with breaded veal or chicken cutlets or meatballs waiting in the folds of the Cut-Rite wax paper.

Not much changed, lunch-wise, when I went to work every day for the next five years after high school. Living at home, each morning my brown bag was there on the table, much like in my early school days. There was the sandwich, wrapped in wax paper, the packaged cake for dessert, an apple, peach or a scored orange, and, of course a napkin.

Curiously, when I returned to work after my honeymoon, the job seemed the same until we broke for our half hour lunch in the break room. Something was underfoot at our little corner of General Foods Corp., but I didn't know what my colleagues were up to.

When I nonchalantly opened my lunch bag with the sandwich wrapped in wax paper, the Funny Bones. My coworkers tried not to be obvious as they craned to see something. Maybe they were looking for my gold band? Would I take it off to eat my lunch?

And when finally I unsuspectingly lifted the napkin from the scored orange, a raucous cheer exploded. My coworkers had wagered whether or not my new wife scored my lunch bag orange as my mom had for years.

Nowadays, I make my sandwich each afternoon as I remember but there's nothing write about. It's just a sandwich, green tea and something by Jane Austen, or based on her work, such as **Master Under Good Regulation**, a guy-dog story, to read. And, I could never think of anyone who would want to read about my humble lunches through these decades.

Scouts seek nudist camp over the mountain

Solo-Suzuki, Locket, me and the rest of our small scout troop followed Hiney through what passed for a trail skirting the swamp end of Wildcat Lake, trudging up the side of a mountain in search of the nudist camp just over the hill from our scout camp.

Hiney knew from other scouts that if we went over the mountain we'd find a road and from that road it was a short walk to the nudist camp somewhere near Blairstown, where anything could happen to pubescent boys.

This was the second week of our stay. The first week of summer camp was typical scout stuff.

The nature trail had several different kinds of pine trees you could determine by the number of needles in a bud. You followed a colored plate on the tree and that kept you on a trail. A counselor would explain what you were looking at. "It's much more than a tree, it's an evergreen pine tree," and such.

Mornings were spent making lanyards out of leather or carving neckerchief holders into Indian heads or arrows, the kinds of artwork that make a Charlie Brown Christmas tree a family treasure.

Afternoons left time to swim in the lake. If you didn't swim, you had to learn before camp ended. You got to practice your swimming in the crib. It was a dock with a floor and resembled a wooden built-in pool at the edge of the lake.

To prove you could swim, you had to do a couple of laps in the crib without stopping. Then the real proof came when you jumped in the lake, into water over your head, and swam around.

Our scoutmaster said that if we didn't learn how to swim after the first week, he'd paint our nose red with mercurochrome. I knew there would be one kid who would never jump in water over his head no matter how many weeks he was at camp.

At night we sang songs at a bonfire alongside the lake and heard Taps played from the turret at 9:45. Some of us listened to WMCA or WABC on a transistor radio for news of faraway New York.

It was a long hike to the south side of the lake where a guy named Nimrod was our instructor at the rifle range. We learned how to shoot .22 rifles. There was one shooting post where it was x-ed out because of a rock on the berm. Otherwise, we got to take a few shots lying down and in a sitting position. That followed Nimrod's safety class before anything else. (Who knew all shooting instructors were called Nimrod?)

Other days we learned how to left-face, right-face and about face as part of our paramilitary training. We could take a row boat out if we could swim. I fished from the shore

But most of us were there for the fun of living in tents in the woods and watching campfires and learning to live off the land. If you showed excellence you might be invited to the Jamboree to show off your stuff.

That second week our regular scoutmaster went back to work and we had a fill-in.

So, one morning after breakfast our troop packed up and followed Hiney, our Explorer, heading west past the swamp end of Wildcat Lake, over the mountain in search of the nudist camp.

By Tuesday morning, it didn't bother me when strange campers asked me about my red nose. "I got a bloody nose."

Nobody along for our hike mentioned my nose, but I could tell every once in a while someone would be looking over at me. Maybe one kid with a red nose would mess up our chances at the nudist camp?

Hiney did a good job getting us over the mountain and at the bottom of the woods we found a blacktop road and headed south. It was already getting hot and we felt like we had gone very far.

The map showed a creek off to the west and we headed through a farmer's field. We got to the river and although it wasn't a huge wide river, it might as well have been. And anyway, none of us had brought along swim trunks. Who would think to bring swim trunks to a nudist colony?

Some of us stripped down (everyone but me) and jumped in the water, swimming and splashing.

I needed to be persuaded to strip to my briefs and wade in.

All I could think of was those cartoons where the animated character is drowning and each time he comes up for one last breath, he counts one, two, or three and meanwhile sees all the events of his life passing before his eyes.

When I suddenly stepped off bottom into deep water, the world went strangely quiet and I tried to hold up one finger for ONE!

I should have thrashed and screamed and called out. Instead, I went down a second time. My nose pushed out again into the air and I held up two fingers this time for TWO!

Starting to worry that my anti-learning to swim would be a hindrance in this western New Jersey river, the third time I called to Hiney as I thrashed and showed him three fingers beyond my red nose.

We found a trading post not too far down the road where we bought some lunch and decided to head back. We never did find the nudist camp that day. We hiked back along the road and turned into the woods heading up the mountain between us and Camp Mohican.

Strolling into camp, grown men asked us our troop number and who we were. Our small group had become popular in just one day. "Here they are! They are here," the men said.

Imagine how popular we would be if we found the nudist camp! Man, oh, man.

The grown-ups were not happy with us. We had missed lunch. And when they saw our troop table was empty at dinner, they figured something was up. We were just kids.

We didn't know you had to ask permission to go for a hike. We didn't bother to mention the nudist camp we never found, or the near mishap in the river.

Bob Dylan in Belleville

Jay says he's got the latest Dylan. Debbie says she likes him, Dylan. They look at me. "What about you, Anthony, you like Dylan?"

I formed my hand into a six-shooter and drew from my invisible holster, getting the drop on them both here in Art Class, "Gunsmoke! Yeah!"

No, not that Dillon, that's Marshall Matt Dillon, they said.

"Not the Mister Dillon, Mister Dillon, limping Chester guy?"

We're talking Bob Dylan. The singer. The Blowing in the Wind guy. You heard Like a Rolling Stone, right?

"Yeah, they sing all those Beatles songs. The skinny guy with the fat lips?"

No, that's the Rolling Stones.

"Well, isn't a rolling stone like a rolling stone?"

Jay says he has every Bob Dylan album.

"Oh, that Bob Dial-Ann, I always confuse him with Thomas Dial-Ann," I finally confess.

This is what we talk about in Art Class in Belleville Junior High School.

Years later I find myself writing for the school page of the local Belleville, N.J., newspaper under the late, great editor and friend William Hamilton – a descendent of our country's first treasurer or vice president, or something like that.

So, there we were, a bunch of eager, naïve high school kids who thought we could write something that would get the townsfolk to actually vote to pass the school budget. I wrote a (thankfully) long-lost piece based on George Harrison and the Concert for Bangladesh record. The budget didn't pass, but I was hooked by one-quarter of that two-disc vinyl set that held Dylan singing Dylan tunes -- Mr. Tambourine Man, Just Like a Woman and others. Haven't looked back since.

Now, if on his many travels up and down the coast from Point A to Point B, Bob Dylan had taken any more notice of the working class neighborhoods he might have ridden by on Route 21, well, some of those familiar songs may sound a bit different today.

What if when Dylan visited him, Woody Guthrie was in Soho, the isolation hospital across from School 10?

Dylan may have peeked through his back pages and out Woody's back window and fallen in love with the birdies in the trees, and cherry blossoms falling like snow in the park grounds. Heck, who knows, Dylan may have put down stakes for a while, penning "Highway 21 Revisited" with such songs of local flavor as

Sad Eyed Lady of Branch Brook Park

Talkin' Red Star Yeast Factory Blues

Slow Train Don't Run Behind Muscara's Music Store No More

Girl From Second River

Wallace & Tiernan Pumping My Love to You

(Ain't Gonna Work On) Plenge's Farm (No More)

Silver Lake Girl

High School Sinkin' In The Bog (for Lonesome Joe)

Ballad of the Belleville Valley

Music From the Red Shingle

Bad, Bad Buddy (Beat You To a Pulp)

Tunnel to Freedom (Under the Old Dutch Church)

Who knows what other local musicians could have fallen under Dylan's spell had he lived in our town for a while? Would have been nice to hear Denise Ferry, Peggy Santiglia and Arleen Lanzotta, aka The Delicates, sing backup on a few of his tunes.

And Susan Narucki could have done some fantastic operatic versions of Dylan classics. Her brother John would have gone apoplectic rushing to get his own basement tapes made. And could you see Joan Baez beaten out by the release of "Connie Francis Sings Bob Dylan"?

Heck, the Four Seasons included Don't Think Twice on "Edizione D'Oro".

Instead of hooking up with The Hawks, maybe Bob Dylan would have rocked with Mark V band members Lon Cerami on lead guitar, Tony Montanino on bass, Richie Eder on drums, Ron Hackling on keyboards and George Snow on rhythm guitar. Now, those guys rocked the '60s (and some of them are still rocking today).

Would My Chemical Romance have a different sound had Mickey and Gerald Way and that other kid from Belleville grown up listening to Dylan playing out on the fire escape of the Rossmore boarding house? And catching his midnight shows down the block at the Capitol Theatre?

In April 1975, when John Narucki and I met Allen Ginsberg at Rutgers Newark, the famous poet recalled the trains that ran through the industrial parts of Belleville. But that's about as close as Belleville ever got to being in a Dylan song. That's one less mention than Ashtabula.

Since Dylan probably never even stopped for gas in Belleville, or stayed at a Belleville motel when performing at NJPAC, we can't depend on the man who celebrates his 70th birthday on May 24, to sing the songs of Second River. Guess that means it's up to me...

Flashback, summers and Suntan Lake

Where do lakes go when you grow up? I suppose they grow larger and clearer as you get older. And the times spent there grow from lazy afternoons to full summers half a lifetime ago.

It is as if those brief half-day visits to that far away lake take on a life of their own in the transition from a childhood memory to an adult's memory of childhood.

Some 30-odd summers ago, the children on my dead-end street spent evenings playing Sputnik, a form of dodge-ball, or chasing the Mosquito Man through the sweet smelling cloud of DDT. On carefree summer days we explored the natural spring in the field near the pipeline beneath the power lines, we called them high-tension lines.

Summer TV was different then, you know. There were only a few channels and very few people owned expensive color TV sets. I grew up watching the Three Stooges, Our Gang, and the Bowery Boys or East Side Kids.

Most of these shows would be deemed too violent for today's kids. We had Officer Joe Bolten who showed us the Three Stooges shorts and told us not to do that kind of stuff at home. And even though we knew all the dialogue and all the plots from all the shows because we'd seen them over and over and over again, we labored to watch them on our black and white sets.

Dad nearly disowned the Three Stooges and me. He got to the point where if I watched the Three Stooges one more time, he would have thrown me and the TV out of the second floor window.

Luckily for me, the grown-up guy next door, Benny, enjoyed the Stooges. He invited me to his house to watch the show every day. It provided a half-hour of peace for my dad and Benny had someone other than his wife Rosie with whom to watch our favorite show. Benny was also known as Bruno, I don't know why.

Dad and Benny were kids together in these same houses. They had been neighbors for over 40 years. Neighbors have a way of knowing the right thing to say. Benny's parents spoke in Polish to my grandparents who only spoke Italian. The neighbor on the other side of Benny's house only spoke

Greek. Ironically, in the old neighborhood there were few misunderstandings.

Benny's brother Mitch was Dad's best friend. They had not only grown up together, but they both raced homing pigeons for all that time, too. Mitch's wife Helen was Mom's best friend. The guys had their boids, and the ladies had their bingo.

The guys would sit around drinking coffee, smoking unfiltered Camels or Lucky Strikes and relive memorable pigeon races. As friends with children would, the ladies would gab about what their pigeon-bingo orphans were up to lately.

The kids in the neighborhood had to sweat it out when one memorable day each summer, Mitch gave up his blue Chevy so Helen could drive Mom, the girls, and me to a place a million miles away called Suntan Lake. It wasn't an official summer without one day trip to Suntan Lake in Riverdale, New Jersey.

Helen and Mom sat up front and chatted all the way. The girls, my sister and Helen's three girls, talked endlessly about anything. When we finally got there, Helen and Mom staked out a place under one of the few trees in the place.

The girls, Lulu, Patricia, Mary Ellen and Gloria were off wandering and set off to swim in the deep water. As the youngest, I hung out in the shallow end trying to find the water jets that fed the lake from the bottom. I let the stream blast through my toes and whatever toys I had with me.

Patricia was the most outgoing of all us kids. Before long she had checked everybody else at the lake. In short she knew just about everything about just about everybody who was there that day.

And, of course, they were all her friends. She came back to us and tried to convince my sister and me to say that we were her cousins, as if that official relationship could possibly make us any closer than we already were.

Nobody ever asked if we were cousins, but Patricia wanted us to say we were. She was always thinking of stuff we could do and people we could talk to and other things that mostly made the day trip to Sun Tan Lake zip past.

We piled the last dry towels on the Chevy's seats and sat in our wet bathing suits for the endless ride home. All of us full of the joy of a beautiful summer day in the country, but all so much quieter.

Summer days are made of memories that last a lifetime. Those memories comfort and shield us from the depths of dark waters swirling in the reality of the rest of the year. It has been about 40 years since our last trip together to Sun Tan Lake, but this is the first summer Patricia is not here to share the memory.

Yet her perky, driving drum and bugle spirit and legendary giving of more than she ever had to give, her consistently touching the hearts around her, will be with us always and forever. If anyone asks, we'll tell them we're cousins from Sun Tan Lake.

No Christmas

Sleepless nights of forgotten dreams that never met the light of day. Youth is wasted on the young, it's said. Generations are separated by lingo and basic understanding of fundamentals. Lost in waves of rushing society, clouds alienate father and son.

Saturday morning TV keeps a moral hidden for the end of the show. It's a child learning about life while unaware a lesson is being taught. Fooled again, you might say. Like the time my parents said there would be "no Christmas this year". And I knew it was because dad hasn't worked for months.

Yet, on that gossamer morning, shrouded in silent sadness, being as strong as a little boy might be because the folks don't need a crybaby. Being strong for someone else * perhaps the best gift of the season that might have none. On that morning below sparkling multi-colored balls dangling in green splinters are presents, more presents that I could have imagined. Some wrapped brightly, some already open on the floor beckoning for play.

A surprise like learning without knowing it. This joy overflows for days and days. Then the fun is gone when a school bell pops the bubble of home. The child in me is swiped away to learn with regrets. A futile plea, "Home would be more fun!? And there's the TV Guide for reading. . ."

Dad was a child in the 1920s. He spoke of roaming the hills of Cedar Grove hunting for food and furs. Pointing to houses, "I used to catch muskrats there. . . A long time ago. . . No houses then. . . Just a creek."

Dad noticed my puzzled look. I can't understand where it went. Dad sighs, "I used to go swimming in the Passaic River and none of the other kids ever believed I could touch bottom... I'd dive down and come up with a hand full of mud."

So many times I pinched my nose closed as he drove us across the Passaic River. Some day, I thought, I would drive across clean rivers.

Dad said his friends and he swiped peaches from Plenge's Farm on Joralemon Street. After they'd filled their bellies, they'd skinny-dip in the

Second River. It was clean then and a place for kids to laugh and play. He laughed when he remembered how one of his friend's sisters came by and hid their clothes as they were buck-naked in the creek. He said they had to wait until it was dark to go home.

Dad sighs again. "There's no place for kids to have fun today." Sure, there are playgrounds and Eagle Rock Reservation, but gone are the unsettled parks of god from this town and every town for fifty miles around.

There's congestion in the streets and pollution that turns a child's eyes red. The skies are blue, sometimes, but mostly they're a hazy shade of gray. The stars at night do not seem so bright and they hide from view behind a stream of smoke a skywriter might leave.

But the messages are different. No one's being asked to vote for so-and-so, or buy a piece of the rock. The messages in tonight's skies reveal a choking message, a note of gloom that doesn't promise a sky tomorrow night.

Deterioration of the sky, houses where opens spaces used to be, learning without realizing it! Concrete where trees were, a street where a stream once flowed and the fishes swam and the birdies drank. It's a nightmare that doesn't disappear in the morning.

Kids daydream about astronauts and walking the cracked pavements of the big cities. It's hard for young people to dream about blue skies, green trees and clean rivers. To find azure aqua tufts, frolicking foliage and buck-naked kids swimming in crystal cascades, one must look into my father's memories.

How many hammers is enough?

Strange, it is, to sense the memories that suddenly swim to the surface like the picture in my head of my father as the rag tag kid who swam from the bottom of the Passaic River with a handful of mud, "See, wise guys? I really did swim to the bottom!"

Dad was a good swimmer, a very strong swimmer. It's not an inherited skill. It wasn't until my late teens that I knowingly approached water that was deeper than my Adam's apple. Swimming is something a dad should teach his son before the boat starts to leak.

Building things was Dad's claim to fame. He never took complete credit for a building or a house, but he earned his pride in a job well done. His pride was of a true craftsman who looked back every time and said, "I built it with my own hands and tools. No one could have done it better."

I absorbed his patience and his sense of poetic justice, maybe from just being around him, definitely not from direct tutelage. He did not teach with words - and questions always seemed to annoy him.

"Geeze, that kid asked two million questions," he lamented after a neighbor's child finally went home. The kid had found Dad's homing pigeons fascinating. "Sure, you got to ask questions," Dad said, shrugging his tired shoulders. But Dad won't be remembered for his patience with little kids, especially me. He was a good guy.

When someone picked on one of dad's friends, a fairer man could not be found. He swung a twenty ounce hammer two thousand times a day and had arms as strong and tough as a jackhammer. Most often, his hands kept the peace rather than ended it.

He gave everyone whatever break he could, especially if the guy had a good sob story. Mom always chided him, "Ange, I don't see anyone giving you a break when you're out of work for months at a time."

He would look at her like a man who had just found his kid brother without a nickel in his pocket. "But Ree Ree," he'd say. It was his way and I do not think he ever regretted it.

It wasn't until I bought my own house that I wished I had seen more of the way he worked. When I was a child, the times I helped him seem to all be the same.

"Hold this board for me, Ant, while I saw it. Where'd you put my level? Ya feel like cleaning up here for me?"

The day we installed the drop stairs for my attic, I was trying so hard to be the carpenter he had been. I was trying to do in one day what he'd had 40 years to master.

I finally asked why all the nails I was hitting were bending, yet his drove straight and true.

"Let the vibration quit," he wheezed, his lungs nearly consumed by emphysema, "before you hit it again."

So I did and it worked. I was like a child with a new toy. I found new relish in my labor. I just wanted to drive nails all day. One little lesson Dad taught me made me feel so good. I wondered though, why it took twenty-four years to learn to drive a nail. All I did was ask, and he told me.

I WAS AWED by Dad's garage. On Carpenter Street in Belleville, our old house had a great side lot and a huge garage. In the back of the side lot he planted tomatoes and I sold them, three pounds for a dollar, in the neighborhood from my little red wagon. The garage was big enough to park ten cars before he built in the pigeon coop. Even after the coop, four cars would have easily fit in there. Not that anyone ever parked a car in the garage. We had been so long without a garage, it rarely occurred to us to park cars in it.

Dad customized the red brick building to accommodate the necessary carpenter's tools. The garage itself became a collage of his life. Shelves were filled with every part of his life. Dad had enough tools to put a hardware store to shame. He acquired them by buying one tool here, a kit on sale here, and another one on sale there. Over and over until there wasn't much more he needed for any job.

One of the original tools was a table saw. It was later replaced by a radial arm saw. I had so much respect for these machines that I never turned them on. A saw sharpener found its way in from a garage sale somewhere and so did a drill press. Dad put up shelves for cans of nails and jars upon jars of nuts, bolts and whatnots that had no place under miscellaneous.

Along the floor, half kegs of different sized nails lined up for more than twenty feet. Suspended from the overhead rafters hung sheets of plywood, corner moldings, pigeon crate dowels and rolls of tar paper.

Dad had a different wooden tool box for every job. He built the best tool boxes. They were sturdy, yet not so heavy that when loaded with tools they could not be lifted by above average carpenters. He had even built a fake tool box. It looked like a regular tool box from a distance, but close up, it had six compartments for different penny weight nails.

"Last night, somebody broke into the tool shed at work," he said at dinner, "took all the tools we had there."

"How did you work today without any tools?" I asked.

He paused to decipher the question. "Whoever had some tools in his car passed them around. Most of the guys just leave their tools on the job instead of carrying them back and forth every day. Then, again, some guys work side jobs. As a rule, those guys keep tools in the car. Whenever I have a tool box in my car - I've always got an extra hammer or two. You can never have enough hammers.

"When I don't work, I don't get paid. It's that simple. If nobody has any tools, then we all lose the day's pay."

The hand tools were the carpenter's own; the power tools were the contractor's. It didn't matter one way or another to the thieves, they usually stole whatever they could carry.

Cardboard drums of pigeon feed with screened cut-outs for ventilation lined up like sentinels in the garage outside the entrance to the coop. Inside, the birds watched for the familiar face, the familiar jacket and the familiar hunched stance of the man who fed them, the man they thought was God on earth.

These birds flew at more than a thousand yards per minute from one to five hundred miles away to return to the home Dad provided for them in his garage. Their mates were here, their nests were here, and so were their eggs or squabs.

His 'boids' took baths in flat water pans on our lawn. They ate gravel between the grass blades. Their oil-slicked necks glistened under summer's sun. A hundred pigeons lolling around the water like a Roman orgy.

Dad knew each bird, who its parents were and how well they had flown. He knew what to expect from each racer by its pedigree and whether to keep it alive through winter to the spring Old Bird racing season. A bird that did not perform in races as it should have would have its neck wrung behind the closed garage door. When we figured this out, us kids would stand outside crying.

Even the dumbest homing pigeon was smarter than a roof rat or statue squatter. "Take one of those wild birds ten miles away and you'll never see it again."

Dad trained his birds by taking them on short trips to fly home, and then driving further and further each week until they knew how to get home from at least ten or twenty miles away.

Most of the time the birds would be home at the coop waiting when he pulled in the driveway with the empty crates. I went along for the ride many, many times, counting telephone poles and winking back at truck drivers high up in their rigs at traffic lights. That was long before CBs came along.

On the south course we'd train down the Parkway to Route 22 past the Flagship and let them go near the Dairy Queen. In earlier training we'd bring them to Potter's field near the Budweiser brewery across from Newark airport. After he retired, Dad bought a van and trained other flyer's birds. When the gas crunch came, it all went to hell.

Some of the homing pigeons had become old friends of mine. A few of the breeders were more than ten years old. Whenever I found myself with an abundance of patience, I would stoop low in the coop and the birds would feed from my hand. A light pecking and a slight pinch was their way of telling me when the food was gone. If I would be kind enough to allow, they would eat my freckles.

I learned at a young age how to hold a pigeon so it would not fly away. Grasp its legs between the middle and ring finger, palm the tail between thumb and forefinger. A bird in this position is fairly helpless. I could turn it over. I could hold it close. I could pet it. I could study the rainbow colors on its neck.

Before a race or training flight, Dad checked the band number on each or both of the bird's legs. He had put the permanent metal band on the leg when the squab was small enough to cry for its mother and old enough to raise its wing in defiance to Dad.

For twenty years I competed with those birds for Dad's attention. I knew them well. I knew a blue bar from a checker, and a dark checker from a red bar checker. My favorites were the blue bar splashes. They looked like an average pigeon that had perhaps straddled under the ladder of a sloppy painter.

My favorite pigeons were the little Judas birds. With their wings clipped the Chicos were thrown up to flutter to the coop. That would encourage the racers to land sooner. The Chicos were docile, and smaller than the homers, and could get lost two blocks away.

Although Dad quit smoking years earlier, the damage had been done. The fine white pigeon dust did him no good. It had gotten too difficult to properly train them. And though he never said it, he knew I wasn't interested in it being a family tradition. He agreed reluctantly to close up the coop and sell the birds and all his supplies at an auction. There, I went out and got milk when the supply ran low.

Dad sold his pigeons and retired. He tinkered on his odd little projects. He built collapsible pigeon crates for other flyers. He built a work bench in the cellar because he couldn't take the cold garage in winter.

And he called lots of times to ask my wife and me to come over and kill some time. "You know how it is, Dad, what with the house and lawn and all," I found myself saying a lot, "we'll be over in a couple of days."

When we finally got there, we heard the same song. He bemoaned time we never spent together. Mom admonished, "You decided to have pigeons while your son was growing up. You can't have that time back again."

I never argued. I just waited for him to fall asleep in front of the TV. He slept best in front of war movies and would stay asleep until someone changed the channel or lowered the volume.

Dad liked to go out for breakfast early in the morning, before Mom awoke. She said she would rather sleep until seven anyway. She would tease him about the redheads he really saw instead of just going out for breakfast somewhere. He loved redheads. Whenever he saw one on TV, he would howl, "Hey, Baby Doll!"

He was harmless enough. Just because he was on a diet didn't mean he couldn't look at the menu, he'd say.

THE FIRST TIME my folks had been away alone since their honeymoon in New York City before the war ended, Dad took her to Walt Disney World. He swam in the warm ocean in January. He discovered new neighborhoods walking, gawking like a tourist at the houses wrapped in plastic being termite proofed. He wanted to buy a small house and bask in the warmth under sunny skies.

Mom enjoyed visiting Florida for a vacation, but as for living there for good, she saw only loneliness. All her family was up North. She could see no reason to move there. No reason in the world.

"Why is it so important to move there so soon?" I asked him.

All he said was, "to take care of Mommy."

I thought it mildly amusing that after twenty-six years, he still referred to her as "Mommy" in front of me. To him, I guessed, she always would be.

Somewhere in the Fijis, between blasts of artillery, Dad, before he was my dad, began to smoke cigarettes. A lot of other young boys did. That was war. One of their sayings was, "if you got 'em, smoke 'em."

When the war ended, he kept on smoking, for twenty years, two or three packs a day, no filters, just the finest blend of Turkish tobaccos. His morning coughing shook the plaster and woke the household.

He quit smoking after so many years at the snap of a finger. It was amazing, especially when he let us know how much he had actually smoked. Until then, none of us ever counted, so one cigarette was pretty much like another. The first of the day was the same as the fiftieth – what did we know from how many he had choked down along with sawdust and dirt from his job.

After he quit, he seemed haunted. He sensed an evil justice would grab him and make him pay for the coffin nails he had hammered into his own lungs. Cancer haunted him the way punishment dogs a child who swims in a forbidden pond. Dad knew on the level that somewhere along the line there'd be hell to pay.

IN THE GARAGE, the empty pigeon coop leaks, spider webs seal nail kegs and water leaks from the roof onto plywood stacks. Fighting anger and tears, I dared invade this somber legacy of a man who too late learned he loved me and too late learned I loved him. I felt a shallow, guilty need to account for what had been left behind before time and rust and rot consumed it all.

Why did I decide I had to count a hundred screwdrivers and two dozen hammers, every size plane ever made, and tool boxes up the kazoo? Dad, how many hammers are enough? You've left enough extension rulers to last for my great grandchildren! Would you still walk a mile for a Camel? And, by the way, Dad, I had a little girl. I know you would have loved her. She's a redhead.

A father's place

I wasn't more than five years old the night my father grabbed me with his vise-like hands on his jackhammer arms and swung me over the banister of our second story back porch. Swinging me side to side twenty feet in the air above the concrete sidewalk, Dad and I were having fun. I was safe, safe from the world in his strong hands. My mother's screams of terror stilled my shrieks of joy.

That night, Dad and I bonded – though neither of us knew the lexicon. The image of that night dangles daily in the bittersweet memories my father left me. After nearly thirty years, I can still feel the strength with which he safely held me over the precipice. Little did I know then there was more to a father's place. Now, I have my own daughter, and though I don't tempt fate from a second floor porch, I realize how much there is to this father business.

I am the image my little girl trusts. Everything I do, and everything she sees me do, contributes to that image. I am her trusted friend who knows all and can do all. Those are pretty big shoes to fill.

Dads are the smartest people in the world (after mothers.) Every school day morning I help her study her spelling. She sits on the couch reviewing and I sit in the recliner reclining. When she's ready to be quizzed, she flops the notebook in my lap, "Test me, daddy."

Because she is so good at spelling, because she studies, I like to throw in a word that's not on the list to keep her on guard. In amongst her regular words such as ball, tall and fall, I casually slip in "pusillanimous." After asking me how to spell it, which I couldn't do, we looked it up and she memorized it.

Other times, I help her with her schoolwork but I sometimes take the questions too literally, and she gets them wrong when I tell her to change the answer. She does allow me to check her homework when Mom is too busy.

Dads explain what's fair or unfair and moms decide when it is okay to go out and play. When she tells her friend she has to go in but goes out five minutes later to play with someone else, Dad says how would you feel if they did that to you? She knows how she would feel and pledges not to do it again. But dad knows that she will, and when she does, she'll remember what her dad said. Maybe.

Dads are their children's protectors. Dads chase the monsters out of the closet at night. Dads have a special hug that resolves a nightmare's terror. Dads are as tall as the sky and can reach the cookies moms hide on the top shelf.

Dads have to be dads sometimes. That means they have to yell and maybe spank. Any child can tell you that nobody hits as hard as daddies can. Not even Grandpa. Yet after every reprimand comes the guilt of being a daddy. Dads want to be kids, but too often get trapped into being adults.

Dads are as old as forever. They listen to 'old people' music like Led Zeppelin and the Beatles. Their car radios are set to all-talk stations. Yet, with their own children, dads are forever young. They play horse, hide and seek and checkers when they are in the mood and decide to make time. Dads don't like to play checkers too much because they lose a lot. On a hot summer day, dads will chase you around with a water pistol, and sometimes even let you sneak up on them with the garden hose.

Dads have the largest, strongest hands in the world. Little girls in their cradles tightly grab their dad's index finger and it's as big as the world outside. But for dads, they see that those small hands hold so much. They hold the future and all dad's hopes. They instill the fear of God in Dad when he senses the responsibility in that precious grip.

Dads fix everything. But, what they actually do is take it to their side of the basement and shelve it until everyone forgets whatever it was that was broken.

Sometimes dads can't get out of it that easily. Sometimes dads have to really fix something. That's when the carpenter's glue comes out of the tool closet and the broken gadget sits on the workbench for a few days. When the glue dries, the object is pried off the workbench and nearly as good as new. Dads know that a few gobs of glue will fix just about everything.

It is obvious dads have all the money. He pays for groceries, gas and ice cream sundaes. That's why dad is such a soft touch for a quarter when his little girl helps sweep the sidewalk or does some other task that he'll later redo. A quarter is pocket change to a dad. It is a fortune to his little girl. While mom is struggling with toothpaste coupons at the cash register, Dad is a big spender giving his little girl a nickel for the gumball bandits.

Little girls grow up, as mine has. This year she nailed us on the Easter bunny question. For now, she's not too sure about Santa but she's not taking any chances. We tried to explain that we could never afford to give her what Santa brings. Christmas is a few months off, so whether her blind faith in her parents will last that long is anybody's guess. I am guessing she will humor us through one more season.

She doesn't always humor me.

Enjoy the proud days, come what may, of "that's my dad!" Before you know it, you'll hear, "Who? Him? I don't know him. - Yeah, well, if you don't tell anyone, we - sort of know each other. Okay. Okay, he's my uh- Dad. But don't tell anyone."

When she says she hates me and wishes I was dead, the hours seem like days when we don't speak to each other. Mom asks which of us is the eight year old.

I am a "full-fledged grown up adult, trying to get ahead, trying to get a result," as the song goes. And there's another song that says I'm right from my side, she's right from hers. That's why there are moms. The world needs someone to sort out the mess between fathers and daughters.

Together at breakfast, my daughter and I are like an old married couple. We eat quietly. Pass the milk. Read the cereal boxes. Make goofy faces in the reflection on the side of the toaster. In reflection, I see us differently.

I can offer no protection from the real world, only a way to ease into it. I am little more than a resource to rely on. In order to regroup and gather reserves before striking out again. I can only offer to help her discover what she's good at. On her own she is learning what the world is about. She has her own heartbreaks and her own small triumphs. I can only remind her that there is plenty of time to change her mind about what she wants to be.

Babies are heaven's treasures. They become Dad's treasure. We mold them into our own image – graven or golden – and live with the results.

Dads lift you high, high enough to smear fingerprints on the ceiling, and high enough to test the smoke alarm button. But he can only hold you for so long. Then you are on your own.

The father inside gets me out of jams. He wakes me from my nightmares. He answers my prayers with yeses and nos. He listens to me when I talk to him. He talks to me when I talk to him. He talks to me when I would hear no one. He watches everything I do – his presence always there with me. He hears me when I pray in vain and in earnest. He is the child who is the father of this man. He is holding me while my legs dangle above the bottomless pit of life.

My generation

Does anyone end up in the career researched for his eleventh grade career report?

Really, now? How many future lawyers and future veterinarians wind up working in the factories and warehouses?

We never saw any career reports on "My future in the factory," except maybe by the owner's son.

We all came out of high school loaded for bear. Every eighteen-year-old is immortal, never erring, and ready to grab the world by the tail.

Finish school, get a job, get married, start a family in an apartment. Get a house, then a bigger house. Feel the future snowball on the road to success.

That's the way my generation had it figured.

Reality has a way of cramming its callused hands into our lives: the cost of cars and insurance, high interest rates, income and sales taxes, the incredible cost of used homes - where our left lung is required down payment, and on and on.

Call it shock treatment. Call it a kick in the gut. But going from what we expected to what life has brought to bear has made us all skeptical, if not at least a little wiser.

We were a catatonic generation. We grew up with war on television oblivious for a while to the pain. We saw cities ignite at the match of social unrest. We bandied words like 'environment' and 'ghetto' as if they charted a disease for which the only panacea was other people's money.

Drugs took their toll on the people who sang our songs. Some of our peers perished also. And we wept bitterly.

After so many centuries, we prayed no more to God in Latin. Our iron, stone and steel churches spread their service for the same convenience of Dunkin' Donuts and Seven-Eleven. On Good Friday, the Passion Play churned our insides as we chanted, "Give us Barabbas!'

Helpless guilt boiled from the pit of our bowels. Don't lay that rap on us! We've erred enough on our own.

In droves, we decided to look for God on the street where he lives.

We slammed out of the house thinking we could conquer the world and do everything better than it's ever been done.

My generation is having babies and settling homes. Washed up Jelly-Beaners with half-filled books of trading stamps. How did our parents ever put up with us?

Mine is a generation of strivers, those not among the walking dead, anyway. These kin will always bounce back, will always find a way to adjust personal goals to the real world. The rest fall through cracks in the earth.

Some people of every generation are of the thought that all good things come to those who wait. They put in their time on the job and everywhere else do the best they can and they will be justly rewarded in all things for their honest efforts.

They have faith in human judgment, honest rewards for honest work and the power of positive thinking. Their rewards are not necessarily physical but spiritual and down the road.

Other people understand if they want something they must "Go for it! Get it now! Tomorrow's too late!"

They clamor, claw, pick, probe, pierce and push asunder those who cannot help or who get in the way. The 'gimme guys' are always reaching for the next rung. Their knack for being at the right place is no coincidence, it is in their master plan.

"Either you make it or you don't, but don't be stupid and wait for someone to hand you the world on a tray! You'll wait for nothing."

Twelve years from eighteen to thirty have a way of mellowing out our reckless youth. It gives an entire generation the time to understand the sky may not be the limit but then is that what they really want?

The time comes to readjust our aim from our heart and our minds, to try to point them at the same thing. It is time to settle or strive even harder.

We tend to see how much we do and do not want material wealth. We see how fast ten years can pass, how reunions can never be as sweet as recollections. School was only what we made of it. Life is the same way, it just takes some generations longer to learn.

On outliving two classmates

There is no joy in the news that another Belleville schools classmate has gone on ahead of Judgment Day and me.

It brings back that sunny afternoon in 1969 or so, when our class returned late one afternoon from one of Mr. Forte's field trips.

The school buses had long gone and everyone needed to make their own way home.

A tall skinny friend, Jay, and I walked up Holmes Street. I was going to catch the Public Service bus at Union Avenue and he was going to walk the rest of the way to his garden apartment off Belleville Avenue.

About a block from Union we caught up with Mike and Frank and a few of their hooligan friends.

They were all laughing loudly which is what most hooligans do when they get together.

Then Mike, the beefy kids, says to Frank, the skinny kid, "I'll give you a quarter to punch him in the face."

"Sure!" Frank then pops me in the jaw with his bony fist.

"Give ya another quarter to punch him in the face!"

"Sure!" Frank yelled, and then popped Jay in the jaw.

The tough kids all laughed. Jay and I stood there. Our cheeks stinging, embarrassed, not sure what to do and being outnumbered by the rough kids.

Sure, I knew kids from my elementary school who now, or any time, actually, I could call in to rectify this situation. But they were nowhere around. And these hoods couldn't have found two nicer kids to intimidate.

"I can't believe that you did that," Mike said. "Give you a quarter to hit 'em again!"

"Sure," Frank said, hurling a sucker punch at me and then another one at Jay, as their friends surrounded us.

Frank was wiry and Mike was stout. If either Jay or I was the scrappy type, we could take on that bony Frank and probably outmaneuver lardy Mike.

But, alas, Jay and I were the good kids, the quiet kids, the ones who meekly did their own work and kept our noses clean. We made our parents proud. And we never told them about stuff like this.

You know that Frank and Mike never worried about any of that stuff. By sixth grade, Frank already had a reputation in town. He went to another school in another part of town and kids at my school already knew about him.

They had their pals and we had ours. And except for a few flukes such as this, our worlds never intersected.

Finally, Frank got tired of smacking us, or Mike ran out of quarters, or both. They let us pass, I to the bus stop and jay up the hill and south.

Jay and I never talked about that afternoon. From then on we were mostly cordial when we met.

Frank went on to become a nurse, of all things. Michael went into business. Long after, I met him one day at Burger King in Nutley, where the Grand Union used to be. Mike was behind the counter trying to help out. But he was out of place. He may have been a manger or even the owner for all I knew, but he was only messing things up behind the counter and much to the annoyance of the folks paid to do that job.

It seemed he was trying to treat me special, like you would do with an old friend who brought his family to your new restaurant. Or maybe he didn't even remember me? I was cordial, but I've never forgotten the quarters.

Michael died a few years back. He was in his forties. Frank died recently, in his late fifties. Jay is still around somewhere local. I never run into him. I'm not all that sure I'd know him after forty years. He doesn't do reunions.

Now, I don't know much about the Judgment Day stuff, but it looks like Jay and I inherited the earth, at least for a little while.

Monk's castle joyrides

We passed a new milestone in my household when school started this month. It feels more like a millstone around my neck as I think of the tremendous change in lifestyle it will encompass.

The high school where my 15-year-old is a sophomore has decided to take away her health class and, lo and behold, give her driver's education classes for a semester.

As the father of a little girl who has not missed a day of school in about nine years, I must protest that she continue with health classes and stay as far as possible from any class involving driving the family automobile.

All right, so her driver's education class does not involve actually getting behind the wheel of an actual automobile. The mere thought of my child, the little red-haired tot I once held in one hand, driving a car is enough to turn the rest of my hair gray.

She has relayed that if she passes the written test in her driver's education class, she can use it to waive her written test at Motor Vehicle Services when she applies for her driving permit. How did it come to this? Whatever happened to that little girl who cried when I drifted off to a corner to build something with her Giant Loc-Blocks? How can that little girl possibly even think of driving a car?

I have not grown so senile that here in my 40s I cannot remember when I took driver's education classes in high school. There seemed to be a prerequisite for all driver's ed teachers to have had a gazillion accidents. It seemed that every time they spoke of an accident, it was as if the teachers themselves had the accident. That applied to nearly every accident the instructor discussed, including the ones where no one walked away.

But driving was different when I learned to drive. First of all, the cars were all bigger back then. Plus a lot of them had things in them called seat belts, which some of even wore on the occasions we remembered they were there. This, of course, I would explain to my daughter as learning to drive in the dark ages when I was a teenager in the 1970s.

"Yes, dear, we did have cars when I was in high school. . . . No, dear, it was long ago, but there were no dinosaurs around when I learned to drive . . . except for the Sinclair dinosaur. No. Never mind. There were no real dinosaurs when I learned to drive."

In the early 1970s, it was fun to drive. The speed limits were 60, 70 M.P.H. and higher on some roads. We could pile into the car and go to the drive-in restaurant, or the drive-in theater, where they showed a movie on a giant screen and you watched it from your car.

Then you could go to the food shack and pay an enormous amount of money for some lousy food, no, there were no video tapes then, or VCRs. If you wanted to see a movie without commercials, you had to go to a theater.

But I digress, as Stephen Daedalus used to say.

Driving was great in the early 1970s. You may not believe this, but gasoline was about a quarter a gallon for the expensive stuff. No, really, I'm not making that up. We could fill the tanks of our old gas guzzlers for about eight bucks and drive for a week.

When we got our licenses, we'd put our money together and fill the tank and drive around and around and around and then around some more. Sometimes we'd get together with whoever we were hanging around with at the time and take a ride to Albino Village on the Nutley-Clifton border. Or we'd head up to the Claremont Diner and check out Monk's Castle. Somebody told me they call it Kip's Castle.

No, they weren't night clubs. The Albino Village was a place I never actually saw. But we planned to go there a lot of times. You see, you take this road along the river, go over a bridge then down a long road and then under a highway, and after you come out of the underpass, that was where everybody said the Albino Village was.

Everybody knew that if you went into the underpass, you had to go to the end before you could turn around. And the only time we ever heard about somebody who went to Albino Village was when they came back and told us about how scared they were and how lucky to get out before they were grabbed by the Albino people.

But I was at the Monk's Castle, once. I don't remember who drove, but it was probably Jerry in that great big Pontiac he drove, with Louie and Cindy and maybe Cathy and her sister Colleen and Barbara and me one day after Thanksgiving.

We parked the Pontiac and headed to the abandoned building that did look like a castle. It was scary, like you see in the monster movies where some brave kid says, "Let's go in!" And all his friends are saying, "Right!!! You go first."

That's the kind of movie where the girl escapes to write a best-seller about it. Really, all we knew about this castle was what we had heard from the other kids.

Undaunted, we tarried up the hill for a closer look, passing signs that said, "Keep Out" and "This Means You Kids," that caused us to tarry even slower.

The dry autumn leaves crunched like church bells under our sneakered feet as we approached the abandoned building. It looked a lot bigger from far away, but as we approached it, it lost its mystery. There was no one here, and no one to chase us away from a closer look. But here in the daylight, it wasn't nearly as frightening as the stories we had heard.

And that reminds me . . . the stories my driver's Ed instructor told me about being on the road were not nearly as scary as really being out there driving responsibly with a load of people in the car.

What is most scary about all this driver's ed stuff is that a long time ago, Cindy and Louie got married and their son, little Louie, I guess, is probably out on the road right now heading with his friends to Albino Village or Monk's Castle but, of course, not with my daughter, who will be taking an extra semester of health classes from now until she's 30.

Do we ever stop missing our folks?

Grandma called Mom every night at 6:15. Every single weekday this went on for years and years, from before I was born, I suppose, until Grandma finally moved in with us.

"There's the warden checking in," Dad joked when the phone rang at 6:15. And sure enough, it was always Grandma.

Each evening she and Mom talked about whatever the day had held, what long-distant relative they might have heard from, or what the grandkids were up to. On and on, they talked, every night, and they never ran out of things to say.

When Mom was on the phone with Grandma was a good time to ask for stuff she would usually tell me no to if she weren't distracted. It turned out that from 6:15 to 6:30 was always a good time to ask, "Can I have a pony?" or "Can I go bike riding out of the neighborhood?" or "Can I have a puppy?"

Okay, so it didn't always work. I had to wait until my sister's high school graduation party when there were hundreds of people around distracting her to actually get Mom to say yes to a puppy. Otherwise, when she was talking to Grandma was the best time to ask for something that would otherwise be a certain no.

As soon as she picked up the receiver, I began asking, "Who is it? That for me?"

"Who do you think it is calling at a quarter after six? The Man in the Moon? Hi, Ma. Just give me five minutes peace and quiet. No, not you, Ma."

Then after she hung up, she tracked me down wherever I was and asked what I wanted. Nothing was usually all I could say. But after a night of yelping. I got to keep the puppy, for 14 more years.

A few times Mom would stop on her way to the phone, and say aloud, "I was going to call Grandma and tell her something," but she realized Gram had died years ago. How could she have thought that after so long? What was Mom thinking? But there was nothing to say to Mom. Gram was still alive in her thoughts so many years later.

When Mom was living alone, I visited every night for a few months and put some medicinal goop and glop in her eye. After the late-night application, she'd sit there in her PJs and housecoat and we'd chat or watch TV for a while. No matter how many times I tried to explain about how come Sam Beckett looked in the mirror and saw a woman or some other guy's face, I don't think she understood.

"He went into this time machine, sort of, and he takes over people's bodies and only you and I can see him, but the people in the show only see the person he's supposed to be. Except for his friend Al. But Al is just a hologram, so nobody but Sam can see him. Anyway, Sam takes over people's lives and is supposed to change their destiny. And, well, it's just pretend, Ma, that's all."

She nodded, then tucked in her housecoat. We didn't talk about much, mostly just kept company for a while. "Don't let me miss my numbers. How come when I tune in early they are late and when I tune in a few minutes late, I missed them?"

Then it was home to walk the dog and check on the family.

Now, years since she's gone, I check on my family and walk the dog underneath a starry night. In the silvery sparkles that balance the night's vast darkness, I wonder of holograms and traveling through time to make things right but find no more answers than before. And I think of something I want to tell Mom.

Married to a Christmas nut

At the end of November, my plain, normal, ordinary English teaching wife went mad. She whistled tunes about a fat guy, deer that stand in rain and told me not to be naughty because I was being watched.

She cluttered the breakfast table with holly until I could not find my cereal bowl. Eggnog filled each and every shelf in the refrigerator and all my root beer had been banished to the pantry. I awakened to smell the chestnuts. It was too late to change her or find a cure. I married a Christmas Nut!

As soon as I forked down the last slice of Thanksgiving pumpkin pie into my gullet and licked the plate clean of whipped cream, she began pleading with me to take her to the Town Pub to see their yearly Christmas decorations. I shuddered at the image of what would happen when she finally wore me down. The folks at the Town Pub smiled when we entered but I sensed their apprehension of what she'd do. Her eyes brightened and her jaw dropped when we walked in the dining room.

Lights were strung across the ceiling, down walls, behind specialty beer mirrors and across cash registers. Every other place twinkled challenging the Great White Way. Wreaths of berries and pine cones of every size competed for attention.

Evergreen pervaded the haze of afternoon's cigars. Plastic Santas stared from points of prominence and a sign on a big bag of wrapped gifts says, "Do not open 'til Christmas." I guided her to an empty seat but she could not sit. "I'll nail your shoes to the floor if you touch one piece of tinsel," I whispered behind a smile.

"That wreath is a little crooked," she said, starting to rise to it.

"Look, if they wanted Oleg Cassini or Laura Ashley to help them get Christmas spirit, they would have called them to Bloomfield."

She settled back into her chair and passed the night in wide-eyed appreciation of the season. She would need her winter recess to get that look off her face.

Her 125 students had it much worse than I do. They began their Christmas projects before their turkeys were in the oven.

"Prewrite, write, rewrite. How many reindeer does Santa have?"

"A noun is a person, place or thing. A stocking is a thing. Stocking is a noun. How many presents will fit into a stocking before it falls off the mantel? Mantel is a noun."

"Mickey Mantle is a ball player, but that's not important right now.

"Class, your essay today will be on the best Christmas gift you've ever given someone." And so on, until the children are finally spared by Christmas holiday.

Her classroom makes "season's greetings" cards pale by comparison. In it, she has a Christmas scene painting nine feet long that one of 'her kids' made. Whether or not there was room for more decorations, there are also a green paper tree seven feet high, and two dozen bells, angels, poinsettias and holly wreaths.

When her principal said her room was attractive, he had to be wondering two things. First, he had to think about the cost of custodians' overtime to get back to the bulletin boards. And secondly, he had to wonder if he would ever find the door back to the hallway.

The last time I found the door in our apartment, we spent a week one night driving all around town to find just the right tree to squeeze back through a doorway half its size.

My wife did the pointing, and I did the lugging. Once the tree was secured in the tin watering stand, I held the ornament box while she did the hanging. I tried to help her fill bare spots. I turned the tree so that people on Mary Street could see how beautiful our tree was. She wouldn't stop her ritual until she dropped from exhaustion.

Her favorite way to pass an evening is to turn off all the lamps and stare at tiny blinking lights hidden in needles and tinsel of our live tree.

No matter how perfect I think the tree is, she can always find the one ornament she had the lapse in judgment to let me hang while she sipped eggnog in another room. When she reassigns mine, it knocks all of hers out of sync. She could kill a whole night because of my help. Even at that, she spends hours every night trying to get the light and sparkle 'just right.'

The only thing worse than all the decorating is shopping in crowds of people, who, like me, shop only one month a year. I drove my wife to every store she could think of, but she still could not find everything she needed to finish shopping before Thanksgiving.

She said it was my fault that she didn't have all her shopping done before the seasonal procrastinators. She wondered what she had gotten into when she married me.

"You have about as much interest in shopping as a log does," she cursed me.

I knew she would fall flat any second. How long could such a tiny tiger keep up this pace?

"What a match we make," I said, "the Christmas Nut and the Christmas log-"

She looked about to strike.

"-we could do wonders by a fireplace."

She smiled, took me up on my idea, and Christmas has never been the same.

Of Taylor ham, skorpers and Ashtabula

My daughter returned from a visit that included a stop in Ashtabula, Ohio, to visit relatives. She brought me two souvenirs – a book and some food – from the town where I spent many a mellow, well-behaved teenage summer.

The book was from the national series Images of America, Ashtabula, people and places which much like Nicole Canfora's Images of America - Belleville recaps the town's history through photos and narrative.

My daughter brought back two bags of my favorite bakery treat from my long ago summers, brittle bread slices covered with sugar, cinnamon or whatever. They go great with coffee but sometimes you have to try to break them into long strips so they'll fit in the cup.

As near as I can tell, the only place to get Finnish skorpers is at the Squire Shoppe Bakery in Ashtabula. The store is on Lake Avenue – many streets are named for nearby waters – but I remember the small shop they had on West 3rd Street back in the day.

Thinking my description of skorpers as a kind of sugared toast or hard bread is a tad lacking, I checked it out online where it says it's sort of a cake, at least that's what I think it says.

Here, read it for yourself. Wikipedia: *Gibbery is a skorper or cake wi a ginge gust. As a skorper, gibbery can be made intil a scleff, crisp ceukie (aft cried a ginger snap) or a safter skorper seemilar tae the German Lebkuchen. Gibbery skorpers is aft cut intil shapes, parteecular Gibbery men. No tae be confuised wi the Gibbery-men or Gibbery-Wummen that selt it.*

To the Jersey ear, Ashtabula might sound downright funny. According to my gift book, it translates to "river of many fishes" and the town today is divided by a river running through it. Basically it was Ashtabula on one side and Harbor on the other. They merged about 75 years after the first settlers settled in about 1802.

In the 1930s or so, a distant relative followed the train jobs and settled in Ashtabula, in northeast Ohio. In the mid-1960s, my sister, Lucille, who had never spent the whole night sleeping over next door on Gless Avenue in Belleville, and cousin took a train meet our relatives out west.

The short version is that she left our happy home on Carpenter Street in Belleville and married the Harbor High quarterback. She traded her keypunch operator job at Mutual Benefit in Newark, N.J., for a keypunch operator job at Bula's uptown Carlisle's department store.

In the late 1960s, I got to spend weeks on end at their house on West 13th Street, in Harbor, Ashtabula. One of the first things she noticed when they'd settled in their house was that she couldn't find Taylor ham in the stores, and a good Jersey veal cutlet was a dream.

So, when any of the family or friends headed out, there was a long-distance phone call to see what would fill the cooler during the car ride.

I spent most of my summers on a borrowed bike wandering the numbered streets of Harbor, mostly the west-numbered streets that counted down to the road along the lake. Heading north, after W. 3rd Street comes Walnut Boulevard and Harbor High School, then down the hill to Walnut Beach. Lake Avenue leads to Lake Erie, but doesn't parallel the shoreline at this part of Harbor.

Most of the time I'd spend riding around town on the city streets through the working-class neighborhoods of well-kept homes where the curtains were almost always open. Once in a while I'd head out of town, west on Carpenter Road or cut over on W. 9th Street to pick up Lake Road West where it becomes 531 and head past the Kent State campus towards what used to pass for sin-city or Geneva-on-the-Lake.

Ashtabula in those days was a lot like Mayberry on the TV show, good, hard-working people, but with a different accent. They said I "tocked" funny. I said they "tawked" funny. We were people divided by a common language.

The first time I asked for soda, expecting them to break out the Brookdale, I got a glass of club soda. That's when I learned they call "soda" by "pop". And what made this Jersey boy jealous was that they got their driver's licenses at 15 years old.

Those were summers where nothing happened and it was just fine with everyone.

It never occurred to my teenage brain that my sister and her husband, though still practically newlyweds, now had another mouth to feed, and that was my bottomless pubescent belly.

And, so it went that I'd leave the expensive Coke and Pepsi for the old married people and I'd drink the Kool-Aid or whatever generic mix we had in the house. Part of my job was to empty the pitcher by drinking it, and the other part was to refill it with the mix, tap water (from Lake Erie) and ice cubes when I'd finished the first part of my job.

Those were the days of rotating TV antennas to pull in stations from Cleveland or Erie, Pa. The staple of my mornings was a local treat called skorper. When they were in the kitchen on West 13th, they never lasted long enough to get stale. It was at that kitchen table where I learned the fine art of breaking skorpers on the horizontal so they would easily dunk in a coffee cup.

And now that my daughter brought back a bag of sugar skorpers and a bag of cinnamon skorpers, it's time to pass along the family tradition. That might go great with some Taylor ham.

Who is Brother, who is Uncle Bim?

"If only this kitchen could talk!" Aunt Connie said when I visited her in April. She was 83 and still living in the same house where she was born.

Except for the addition of a kitchen where we sat, a first floor indoor bathroom and a back porch, it was the same four-room house her father, Raffella Aliperto, built for his budding family shortly after the turn of the century.

I had come to learn about my relatives. When my folks were alive, it never occurred to me to sit them down and write all this down. Now, Aunt Connie's memory was to be tested, for the sake of future generations.

The last time a tax assessor came, he wanted her to show him the rooms in the attic. She told him there was no attic. He was adamant as tax assessors are supposed to be. The front of the house had a pitch, and the back of the house had a pitch, therefore there must be a second floor with more rooms to tax.

On the west side of the house is an old garage with a foot of space from her house. It is barely enough room to swing a hammer, let alone look up and see the roof.

The backyard is virtually landlocked with Mr. Edison's plant bordering the rear, and the neighbor on the east blocking other access.

To get to the backyard from the street, you have to go in the front door, through the house and out the back door.

She led the assessor down the hall off the kitchen to the door that led to the cellar stair. He demanded she open it and show her the stairs to the attic.

"There is no attic." She repeated.

When he saw the stairway, he looked for a hidden panel and when he found none, he conceded there was no attic and no taxable rooms upstairs.

"The front and rear roofs pitch to the center where they drain," she explained to the disgruntled assessor, "I grew up here, I should know if there is a second floor."

Raffella and his wife Madeline Penna came from Marigillano, Italy. In Belleville, New Jersey, United States of America, they had seven children and lived in a four-room house Raffella built on Alva Street adjacent to a factory owned for many years by Thomas Edison himself.

The four-room house was plenty. It had three bedrooms; one for four sons, one for three daughters, and one for the parents It had no kitchen, but the Aliperto family never went hungry.

As the work whistles blew and the smoke spewed from the factory in their landlocked backyard, Raffella, like most illiterate Italian immigrants worked as a laborer to support his children, Sam, Celia, Frank, Tom, Dan, Connie and Lucy.

Most of the projects Raffella worked on to support his family are lost to renovations, demolition and long-forgotten memories of a weary father pointing to places he once dug ditches and carried a heavy yoke.

One place where he worked stands today and is pointed out to descendants who happen to Alva Street to ask where Connie's father worked. He helped build Sacred Heart Cathedral in Newark, near Branch Brook Park where each spring Cherry Blossom trees bloom and fill the air with sweet scents and pink hues and petals that may lighten the labor of men like Raffella who came to America to raise families in a better life. The Pope himself said Mass there in 1995.

Aunt Connie's kitchen seemed smaller than I remembered it from my boyhood visits. She wept as she recalled the family, come and gone, good friends and relatives who drank coffee and ate the finest Italian pastries and cooking and chatted the night away for birthdays, anniversaries and for no reason at all.

"It's nice to have someone to talk to," she said, for the moment forgetting Uncle Al, who seems to have been married to her for as long as I can remember. He is as cantankerous at 81 as he ever was.

Together their foils sparks light up lonely nights of tender memories. "Only JoAnn comes to visit. I keep the bills here so she can write them." Aunt Connie raises gnarled hands, "With this arthritis and my stroke, I can't write."

For the longest time Aunt Connie was a part owner of Embroidery Masters on Belmont Avenue in Silver Lake. She and the other ladies did fine embroidery. When my sister Lucille got married in 1967, Aunt Connie presented her a fine-embroidered bedspread. It was a work of art and the envy of the family.

Aunt Connie and Uncle Jim had raised three children here in this house. Uncle Jim died in 1960 at age 56 -- a quirky age that many of the siblings succumbed to cancer. Of his children, Frankie was oldest. He was one of several Frank Cocozzas in the family, all named for my great-grandfather. I knew him as Cousin Frankie in Brazil. His sisters JoAnn and Ria had all boys.

Aunt Connie could name not only her grandchildren but relatives from both branches of the family tree. The Alipertis had grown up with the Cocozzas, so all her life they were one big Italian family. She knew all their stories and could remember them, their birthdays, and their children's birthdays too.

How Aunt Connie could remember. She remembers names, dates, how old dead relatives would be today, what villages in Italy our ancestors came from, which in-laws worked where, how they died, and who are whose children, and where they are today. She had even visited Naples and distant relatives there. At 83, her mind clear and certain, Aunt Connie is a virtual walking encyclopedia of family history.

And as soon as we were settled in Aunt Connie's kitchen, she in the kitchen chair with the pad on the seat and the armrests, me poised with pen and pad, video camera aimed at the table top.

Uncle Al sat opposite me, patiently, uncharacteristically listening quietly as I asked the first question about my relatives. This silly question sparked my curiosity, so, I had to call Aunt Connie and ask to visit her.

"You want me to drop dead?" she said on the phone when I asked if she felt up to a visit. "Are you trying to kill me?" She was, I knew, nowhere mad at me, or feeling threatened, her sarcasm hit its mark. She was the most boisterous of all my relatives.

I tried to remember the last time I had been to Alva Street. When was the last time I had seen Aunt Connie? Neither of us could say whether or not if it was a wedding or a wake. It felt good to sit in a kitchen that held so much history and family and warmth.

On my mother's branch of the family tree she gave me uncles with names that were not their own. For instance, Uncle Jim was Vincenzo, Uncle Butch was Andro, Uncle Lou was George, and Uncle Bim was who knows?

Aunt Connie would know. Uncle Bim and Uncle Lou were her brothers-in-law. The famous singer who took his mother's name for professional reasons was also a Cocozza, although Mario Lanza was not a relative, as far as anyone knew.

But there was one relative I could not account for, Brother. About all I knew about him is that he is older than me, never married and wore a beard. His was the first and only goatee in the family.

"Who is Brother, Aunt Connie? And how am I related to him?" I asked. She sat on the pad in her kitchen armchair, hands folded nearly in prayer, eyes bright behind trade mark oversize glasses ready to answer the most difficult heritage question I could hurl.

She seemed disappointed at the softball I had tossed her. "He's your mother's cousin, my nephew. His mother, Anna Cocozza was your grandfather's only sister. But here's the twist. His father was my brother, Frank Alberti."

When Anna died of cancer at age 56, Brother lived with his father Frank Alberti, and my grandfather's two bachelor brothers Frank and Uncle Bim Cocozza in the family house on 11th Street in Newark.

Who is Uncle Bim?

Officially, Donato was his first name, but he went by Daniel. Being the youngest of the boys, his older brothers would come in from work, or wherever, and give him a penny or other change. It appeared to everyone that Donato "always had money just like the guy in the funnies, you know, Uncle Bim." And so, unofficially, even if he weren't my grand-uncle, I would surely call him "Uncle Bim," just as his brothers had since the Roaring 20s.

On my way home I realized I hadn't asked Aunt Connie one question, and now that I know who is Brother and what his real name is, I should have asked why he is called Brother. Another time, the good Lord willing.

At Spatola's Home for Funerals

Andrew Pagliaro died April 22, last week. He was 93 years old. I never got to talk to him before he died. I have a couple of letters he sent me a couple of years ago.

I keep his letters with a note from New York Times writer Russell Baker who once lived in Belleville and wrote part of Growing Up about life here, and two from Gay Talese, author of *Unto The Sons* and more.

In October 1991, Andrew Pagliaro, age 92, saw my name in an ad for my book A Father's Place in the Italian Tribune. He wrote me a letter and asked me if I was related to Anthony Buccino, the first person he met in America when he came here in 1907.

Andrew said his Anthony Buccino lived at 6th Ave. on the corner of 12th St. in Newark. Andrew and Anthony both went to St. Rose of Lima school. My Buccino family is hard to trace before 1929, and I wrote that as far as I could tell, I was not related to his old friend.

Pagliaro's letter touched me. I am not made of stone. His letter, scratchily scrawled, showed me how moved he must have been to see my name and how touched he was by the memory of a good friend he had when he was seven.

What would I remember from my childhood should the Lord allow me to live to 93? I thought Andy was a sweet, precious little old man.

I sent him a free book. It doesn't end there. Andy Pagliaro is from the old school. On Christmas Day 1991, he sat down and wrote me a thank you note on a half-sheet of lined notebook paper.

At Andy's wake, Spatola's parking lot was nearly empty on a Friday night in April. Spatola's is a grand old funeral parlor on Mount Prospect Avenue in Newark. I walk through empty rooms at Spatola's and remember many family funerals, and my father's in 1980.

Walking into a wake of someone I didn't know to visit his bier I felt uneasy in a pleasant sort of way. I knew that unless I stopped by to tell the story of Andy's letters, his family might never know about his childhood friend whose name was the same as mine, and though probably not related to me, merely seeing that name inspired Andy to remember a good friend from long ago.

Andy was slightly built, with a thin white mustache. His visage reminded me of an old-time Italian barber. He was not a barber. The Star-Ledger said he had been a materials handler for Wagner Electric in Newark until he retired in 1964. With his late wife Helen, he had two children, Gloria and Michael, and five grandchildren. Andy enjoyed retirement for twenty-nine years. God bless you, Andy, and rest your soul.

They say the first afternoon of a wake is for the family and the evening is for friends. When my grand-uncles died, back in the 1960s, wakes lasted two days before the funeral. These days, people want to get on with life, such that it is. Shorter viewing relieves stress on the family, and cuts down expenses.

I did not know Andy Pagliaro except for the two letters he wrote to me. When I turned to face the family, I did not know who to console. I stared, dumbly collecting my thoughts. This was the same room my dad, grandmother and Aunt Julia were laid out in their time.

First I spoke my regrets to Andy's son-in-law, then to his daughter, then to the small group gathered. There was much he could have said about our ancestor's struggles, I said.

They seemed not to know that Andy's first friend in America was Tony Buccino. They seemed a bit surprised that he would have written to someone whose name appeared in the Italian Tribune. Even now, at 93, Andy Pagliaro surprised his family.

I'd like to think that as I quietly exited through the nearly empty funeral parlor that the story of the writer who got a letter from Grandpa Andy was being retold to his grandchildren in the back of the room.

Strangers in old photos

Who are these people in these old photos? The squares look like poster stills from some old WWII movie. They are black and white, somewhat out of focus; yet, these people do seem to be enjoying the moment. It is obvious they enjoy the moment of togetherness that is frozen in time before me on such brittle and fragile paper.

These long-ago relatives gathered at a wedding here, a baptism there, a picnic there. They hammed it up with a smile, or stood prim and proper in a nearly formal pose for all posterity.

In one large photo at a large family gathering, the children sit in front on the floor and the various branches of the family stand nearly together. Even those in service were remembered with empty spaces near their spouses.

The immediate family seemed larger then. The family gatherings were fit for an army and that is what the family seemed when it gathered at holidays, weddings and funerals. But that was before the family became diluted by the new nuclear family with its Interstate Highway System.

My generation was born in the era of Kodak Brownie cameras and black & white film popularity. Four or five decades ago even the simplest camera was somewhat complicated to master.

It is also rare to ever find the designated family photographer actually in a picture. If you look close enough at the corners of some photos you will see not the gathering shadow of a hawk about to make off with our little children, but an errant finger poised in front of the unforgiving lens.

The oldest photos I can find in these cardboard boxes handed down generation to generation are mostly from the post WWII era.

In each family photo, all the relatives are fully clothed. Even the rare photos of great-grandma at the beach, she wears a suit that appears to have more material than today's cocktail party dress.

Young men captured in these photos seemed impressed with their own youthful physiques.

Not that that should surprise anyone, in those days, a day at the beach was no day at the beach, if you know what I mean. So, it is not unlikely that they would relish the relief of the day whether at Sandy Hook or in the Jersey hills near Highpoint or across the river in Coney Island.

Once upon a time there were photos in a long-since-lost shoebox tucked away in rafter storage in the garage. They held someone else's memories of black & white coconut trees in the Fiji Islands.

Also in the faded film were the native women in grass skirts, smiling for the sweating, malaria-afflicted soldiers come to set them free in a world gone mad.

And other photos reminding of the grim reality of those days: young draftees poised with artillery cannon peering through camouflage netting past a tropic tree line at a vast gray blur of ocean.

A few weeks ago grandpa was the subject of an interview demanded by a high school history teacher.

We tried to help our daughter focus her assignment questions.

We could almost predict the answers, but we tried to steer her towards the high points of grandpa's seventy-three years here.

Ask him about the Marines, we suggested, and how he got in even though he was too young. And how he met grandma, my wife added.

And don't forget to ask why he left Pennsylvania and spent the last forty years in Belleville.

Write this down; remember to ask how it was growing up as the baby in the family after his father died in 1929. Ask how grandma made do with all those mouths to feed. She baked bread for the baker, you know.

"Wait. Stop. I can't write that fast," our daughter said, halting the questions. "How could he have done so much? What was that last question?"

Of course grandpa was ecstatic at the undivided attention and keen interest paid by his only granddaughter. She rattled off a question from the list, some ours and some hers, and took notes on his answers.

Then she asked another question, and scribbled some more. Nearly out of earshot, we eavesdropped unobtrusively nearby.

And weren't we all surprised at grandpa's answers. Almost none of them agreed with what we thought we knew about him. And where did those extra questions come from?

We never knew he had a trucking business after the war and before he came to Jersey. How did she even know to ask him that?

The axiom 'little pitchers have big ears' is true when it comes to family histories. Our little one remembers details of grandpa's long ago stories that her mother and I would swear we never heard about in our lifetime.

"Hey," my wife erupted after our daughter had finished her inquisition, "that's not the way I remember the story! You never told me you owned a fleet of trucks after the war!"

Ah, his unit ended up in Tarawa, without him.

"And I didn't know you were a rifle instructor in the Marines!" As an aside, she told me, "Forty-something years you live with these people and they still surprise you!"

"Ain't it the truth?" I nodded. "I guess we all have our own history, however we remember it."

The family history is more than old photographs, and yet it is nothing if not passed along to succeeding generations.

One way to preserve our own history is to set up a video camera on an older relative and keep passing along the decaf and old photos while recording the stories and tales of the relatives and friends in each fragile depiction. It is so easy to put this off until next week that never comes.

Sure every picture tells a story, but not as well as when grandma or grandpa is looking at a frozen moment in time.

That's when you'll hear the stories of great-grandpa cranking up the Model T for a trip down Route 1 to the shore.

Photos of the boys in service and their homecoming tales are surely worth the price of admission. Maybe grandma will tell you about her cousins, the three Veneziano brothers who died separately in the war. You know about the plaque on Newark Avenue, it has their names on it.

Your snippets of family history need not be formally recorded and typed out on the latest fancy computer. It is not, after all, a history assignment.

But some day you'll thank yourself for making the time when you pull out that old videotape and find how cherished those rambling tales have become.

Perhaps the most memorable pictures of family are in the scenes never captured by film yet nestling in the tangled gray matter awaiting a neuron cue to kindle a dormant memory or a spark of recognition.

Anyway, at the next wedding or family party, make sure you catch that Kodak moment with whatever camera you have handy. That will give you something to talk about with your grandchildren in front of that video camera in the next century.

Counting change

The more things change, the saying goes, the more they stay the same.

At our fingertips, and in our car engines, we have computers. In our eyes, we have contact lenses. In our kitchens, we have microwaves. On our desks, we have solar powered calculators. That's change.

On our TVs, we have pictures delivered by satellites. Our music today comes along with a video - we've given up our right to imagine. On our wristwatches, we have no hands, just a dot. We've given up bothering to read numbers. And that watch piece of work goes into a museum! This is the future.

We count our change walking through our neighborhood. No so slowly, but over the years, we have changed. The change encompassed us slowly, one house at a time, one home at a time, one family at a time. We wake up like Rip Van Winkle and look at the neighborhoods around us.

Where Plenge's farm once produced fruit, Rutan Estates produces families.

Where the Milk Bar once served us cold ice cream on hot summer nights, a bank now finances our exotic vacations and our home equity loans.

Where the stately mansions once stood in the valley, now live yuppies in condominiums.

Where tennis courts stood along the beautiful Passaic, now lays the bandit's colorless concrete highway.

Where business bustled on the main thoroughfare, now hope lies smoldering under potholes and shortsightedness.

Where we played in vacant lots now stand condos and housing developments. Wooded lots we spent our summers planning our futures are now some family's lawn.

The Berlin Wall has come down for a generation that knew nothing else. And a way of life here rests in the hands of so few. The way of today is today, with little or nothing for tomorrow. The past is past. There is no tomorrow, only today.

Call for a change. We have to plan ahead. We have to work together. We have to plant seeds today so our children can smell the flowers tomorrow.

Across the seas we hear freedom ring. We see the clips in quick little bursts on the evening news. We have gotten hardened by the glut. It is a changing world. That is for sure. And the old timers will tell you, the countries we beat in wars are now beating us in our pocketbooks.

When we put men on the moon, we left our trash there. The flower children of the 60s are raising skinheads of the 90s.

A baseball player gets a million dollars a year, then goes on strike.

A family lives on food stamps. Another family has no home.

This is the world around us. Here, the more things change, the saying goes, the more they stay the same.

Everybody wants lower taxes and the most services. And we all sit on our back porch watching our taxes go to the county, the state and Washington.

Eventually, we scratch our heads, wipe the cobwebs from our eyes, and have a good look around. What a world. What a world.

And here, in our own backyard, we try to make sense of it all.

We are living in the future. They told us so at the World's Fair. Everything would be easier. Everything would be better. No one would be hungry. Everyone would be clothed. All the diseases would be cured.

Yes, they certainly had the answers to all our questions when we were young. And we certainly believed everything they told us. We were young and wanted to believe.

Now, we seek the answers. We cry out in the wilderness. The answers are not so obvious. We have seen the future, and it is us.

Editor imprisoned in Town Hall

It seemed familiar enough, the new Belleville Town Hall before me. Construction had been completed on the addition in the six years since this building was my beat.

Shortly after the township government changed from commission to council, the steel arrived and the structure rose. Some folks saw the new building and the new form of government as a new beginning as well.

So now the parking lot was different. It wrapped around the north side of the building and exited on Valley Street near where police cars parked.

The place must be humming, I figured, almost all the shoppers' parking places were taken. So I found an open spot, parked and went to feed the meter. It must be my lucky day: the meter was broken and flashed at me in LCD to that effect.

Scanning the new building for an entrance, I spied the garage doors into the police department.

Distant memories of faded blueprints told me this was a sure way into Town Hall.

I proceeded through the overhead doors, past patrol cars parked in the cool shade of the garage. There, ahead, a door marked exit.

It opened easily and I was inside. Where did these stairs lead? All I saw was another set of doors and an elevator.

There was no push button on the elevator door. I pushed anyway. Nothing happened. The last two doors should have been marked "Lady" and "Tiger." I tried one of the doors and it opened.

Finally, I was inside Town Hall.

Or so I thought. I was actually outside again. But not really outside. I was inside and outside at the same time. That sounds about right for a managing editor on the second day.

Above me was a steel grate and dead space above that separated the old Town Hall from the new addition.

So, I was outside the new Town Hall and outside the old Town Hall. Fortunately, ahead of me was the entrance to the old police squad room and detective bureau. I was nearly in. I was so excited to have found my way through the maze as all new editors should. I was excited, that is, until I tried the doors in front of me. There was no handle. They wouldn't open.

Behind me, the solid steel doors I had entered through from the police garage would not budge either.

One door to the left of the glass doors with no handles led into a dark work room. It looked like the kind where the psycho killer spends all his time in those teenage slasher movies. I could think of no reason to go in there.

This part of the old building was underground from the opposite street entrance. Who could tell what danger might lurk inside? And anyway, it was way too dark to have any possible exit.

Off to the right was another glass door into a work area for the custodians. But that door, too, was locked.

Back at the middle set of glass doors without handles, I could hear the plaintive howl of a lonesome dog. And there, up about half a flight of steps, was the plaintive dog, and, much to my delight, a woman from the police records room filing papers.

"Hello," I called. She was startled at first. She probably never expected to see a managing editor trapped in this no man's land.

"What are you doing in there? You're not supposed to be in there!"

I came in from the doors behind me and now I can't get out, I said, rather calmly for a managing editor who has been imprisoned on his second day on the job.

She seemed more concerned that I had gotten into this sacred place than in how to get me out. She tried the doors from her side. Nothing budged. She seemed as perplexed as I was at my predicament.

"Stay there," she said dryly, "I'll call the desk to have someone let you out." She spied my reporter's notebook in my hand.

"You're a reporter?" She said rhetorically. To herself, "How did you get in there? You're not supposed to be in there. That's a secure area." And she disappeared up the stairs of the old Town Hall.

Here, between the old building and the new, was a cornucopia of official government artifacts. Covered in dust but no less protected from the winter's snow was the old Dictaphone 4000 voice recorder that had served to elucidate years and years and years of 9-1-1 calls.

And over here is an old Underwood Touch-Master typewriter, that must have typed out God knows how many police reports using the words "actor" and "perpetrator" in its years and years of service.

The dog howled plaintively. I spied a dozen or so recovered bikes. In younger days, I might have hopped on a bike and done a few laps in my new-found cell, just to kill some time.

Although a nice cool drink on this hot June afternoon would have hit the spot, here the water cooler had no water, merely the accumulated dust of obsolescence.

"The doors are open," the woman called.

Hallelujah, I muttered and headed for the doors behind me. I tried them. They didn't budge. I fiercely grabbed the handle and used all my might and succeeded in snapping my carpal tunnel. The doors held fast.

Back at the glass door without any handles, I spoke plaintively through the missing key hole to the lady again. "Ma'am, I'm still stuck here."

"They told me at the desk the doors are open."

"But I'm stuck here and I'd really like to get out."

"Tsk! I'll call the desk again."

"Thanks, I'd really appreciate that."

In all, the episode seemed to take a month or so to play itself out, but it wasn't more than 15 minutes or so. Finally, two police officers appeared behind me in the no man's land between the old Town Hall and the new. "I hope you didn't let the door shut behind you," I said.

But they had. Now, with the three of us imprisoned here at least I'd have someone to talk to. I could fill them in on where I've been the last six years.

Fortunately, one officer knew the secret of opening the double glass doors without handles and we were on to our business about Town Hall.

All of us, that is, except the dog with the plaintive howl, without whom, I would still be imprisoned in Belleville on my second day as managing editor.

School 10 students surprise Belleville scribe

This was the plan: talk to the fifth and sixth graders at School 10 about going to the school a long time ago when I lived in the neighborhood, then read a poem about growing up, then a poem about the soldiers' memorials, then talk about the 160 men from Belleville who died while in service. Then I'd close with the three men from the neighborhood who perished in Europe during World War II. Maybe the students would come up with a few questions.

But the way these things go, my portion of the presentation finished early even though it included the street name changes at Essex Park on Franklin Avenue, and a reference to the fields where we played before the new housing came along.

Heck, I even told them the story about when my dog Butch followed me to school at lunch time and I had to bring him home and then try to get back to school on time.

One student afterward really, really wanted me to tell him how to get his book in print. He's in fifth grade!

And that other story about my friend Teen Angel trying to ice skate on the pond at the golf course behind Fairway Avenue. He stepped out on the ice in his regular shoes saying, "See, Tonoose, the ice is strong enough for us to play hockey."

But before he could say, "put on your skates and come out," we heard a creaky, cracky sound and veins began to appear in the cloudy skin covering the frigid water below. That's when Teen Angel looked at me and started towards me as the frozen pond swallowed one foot and as he pulled it free, the other foot got sucked into the cold.

A fifth grader called out that we'd have to rescue him like in that movie.

I said, "It's a Wonderful Life?"

And he said it was his favorite film.

We both pictured the scene where George Bailey organizes the other kids to make a human chain to save his brother from drowning in the creek so the brother can later go on to save the men on that troop ship in the Pacific. (BTW, that's where George loses his hearing and later turns up 4F.)

So, before I told them how Teen Angel made out on the breaking ice of the pond at Forest Hills Country Club, or if I actually got back to the ending of that story at all, I asked the young boy, "Do you know who wrote that movie?"

He didn't, but that's okay.

Frances Goodrich wrote the screenplay for that movie with her husband. She was born in Belleville. She and her husband won a Pulitzer Prize for their play The Diary of Anne Frank.

In addition to writing some books and poems about growing up in Belleville and New Jersey, I told them, I've also put together a web site called Old Belleville that has information about famous people from town.

That's when I asked if any of these fifth and sixth graders at my alma mater had a computer. Almost all their hands went up. I tried to explain a computer to children who had never seen an actual typewriter and probably never will.

"You know, it has a tray thing with letters on it..." and they waved their hands rapidly as if I couldn't see them.

"And there's, like, a television screen with it where words and pictures show up?" Ah-ha, they did have computers.

It's easy to remember my web site about Belleville if you look for it on your computer, I told the 10- and 11-year-olds, "Old, like me, and Belleville, like, well, Belleville."

The students listened closely when I told them how many young men from Belleville had died while in the service, fighting wars for our freedom. And then I told them about three neighborhood boys who perished in World War II.

Morris Catalano, 28, of Belleville Avenue, Frances C. McEnery of 34 Fairway Avenue, and Joseph Zecca, 19, of Fairway Avenue, all perished in Europe during the war. I also told them about the Tuskegee Airmen, also known as the Red Tail pilots and a member of that group, Lt. Leonard Willette of Belleville, who perished over Germany.

The neighborhood boys sat in this very auditorium, I told them. Earlier I had explained that as a sixth-grader, I had been on the A/V crew and ran the spotlights and showed the films in what is now the all-purpose room but back then was an elegant single-seat, sloping floor theater.

The neighborhood boys played stickball and football on the same playground as the classes today.

Since I had finished my prepared material, I asked for questions while reminding them that if they ran out of questions, they'd have to go back to class. The children were very interested in the big building across the large lawn. That had been the Soho Isolation Hospital, I explained, where people with tuberculosis, scarlet fever and other infectious diseases went.

That gave me a chance to remind them that where the Essex Park development is was once my playground where we played football, field hockey and homerun derby. Now it's filled with condos and parking lots.

A few students said they live in the development, so I explained that four of the streets are named after Belleville heroes who did not return from the war: William Hamilton, Clatie Cunningham, Carmine Olivo and Raymond De Luca.

The students were eager to hear more of my stories about the knoll on Smallwood Avenue and the friend I made in fifth grade who invited me to his house to eat lunch until we moved into our home on Carpenter Street. And they were curious about students as crossing guards and also about walking all the way home to eat lunch.

My stories must sound so quaint to these pre-pubescents, as if my friends and I had to chase away the dinosaurs so we could play on these cherished Belleville streets. It was a pleasure to share my tales with such an enthusiastic audience.

Remembering Belleville 'Red Tail' pilot

(Jan. 18, 1945) -- Flight Officer Leonard R. Willette, 22, was declared killed in action this week.

Willette had been listed as missing in action since Sept. 22.

He is the son of Newark Police Lt. and Mrs. Lawrence Willette, of Stephens Street, Belleville.

The young man enlisted in the Army Air Corps while a student at New York University. He entered the service from New Jersey.

He refused an appointment by the late Senator Barbour to West Point in order to get into active combat more quickly.

Willette received his wings in February 1944, at Tuskegee Army Air Field, Ala.

He was a P-51 Mustang pilot based in Italy with the famed 99th Fighter Squadron, 322nd Fighter Group, under command of Col. Benjamin O. Davis.

According to W. F. Holton of the Tuskegee Airmen Inc., Leonard Willette graduated from Class 44-B-SE, on February 2, 1944.

Holton says records show that Flight Officer Willette was reported missing in action September 9, 1944, while participating in a combat mission to Munich, Germany.

His last known position was 10 to 15 miles North of Lake Chiem, Germany. He was flying is P-51, Mustang which he named "Wrong Woman."

One of the pilots of the 99th received a radio message from Willette, stating that he was having engine trouble and thought he would have to bail out.

He was at 30,000 feet and losing altitude and his oil pressure was decreasing rapidly.

When the pilot, Lt. Saunders, last saw Willette, he was disappearing through a hole in the clouds at about 20,000 feet.

> ## Belleville Sons Honor Roll
> *A Place of Honor and Remembrance in the Home of the Brave*
> Belleville, New Jersey
>
> ### World War II
> # Leonard R. Willette
>
> **War's Worst Week For Belleville Lists 13 Local Casualties**
>
> (Jan. 18, 1945) -- Flight Officer Leonard R. Willette, 22, was declared killed in action this week.
>
> Willette, service number O1692873, had been listed as missing in action since Sept. 22.
>
> He is the son of Newark Police Lt. and Mrs. Lawrence Willette, of Stephens Street.
>
> The young man enlisted in the Army Air Corps while a student at New York University. He entered the service from New Jersey.
>
> He refused an appointment by the late Senator Barbour to West Point in order to get into active combat more quickly.

A second pilot who was leading the mission, Herman Lawson, was flying at 30,000 feet when he received Willette's radio call that he would have to bail out. The time was 12:33 p.m. on Sept. 22, 1944.

Second Lt. Willette, was awarded the Air Medal with oak leaf cluster, and the Purple Heart, the European-African-Middle Eastern Campaign Medal with 1 Bronze Service Star, WWII Victory Medal, WWII Lapel Button.

He is also survived by a brother Pvt. Lawrence Willette Jr. at Tinker Field, Okla.

He is memorialized at: Plot J, Row 18, Grave 17, at the Lorraine American Cemetery, St. Avold, France.

On Jul. 19, 1941, the Army Air Force began a program in Alabama to train black Americans as military pilots.

Primary flight training was conducted by the Division of Aeronautics of Tuskegee Institute, the famed school of learning founded by Booker Taliafero Washington in 1881.

Once a cadet completed primary training at Tuskegee's Moton Field, he was sent to nearby Tuskegee Army Air Field for completion of flight training and for transition to combat type aircraft.

The first classes of Tuskegee airmen were trained to be fighter pilots for the famous 99th Fighter Squadron, slated for combat duty in North Africa.

Additional pilots were assigned to the 332d Fighter Group which flew combat along with the 99th Squadron from bases in Italy.

By the end of the war, 992 men had graduated from pilot training at Tuskegee, 450 of whom were sent overseas for combat assignment.

During the same period, approximately 150 lost their lives while in training or on combat flights.

Additional men were trained at Tuskegee for aircrew and ground crew duties, flight engineers, gunners, mechanics, armorers, etc. Others were sent to Texas and New Mexico for training as navigators and bombardiers.

Two Nutley sons also served as Tuskegee airmen, Victor L. Connell and Edward Jenkins. They both returned safely to New Jersey.

Italian American roots in Belleville, Nutley

Growing up on the border line of Belleville and Nutley, the children in my neighborhood along Meacham Street knew that when we grew old we would speak Italian. It was as obvious as all of those gray-haired relatives who came to call spoke the dialect.

On Gless Avenue where I grew up, we had a few Polish families and there was one woman who only spoke Greek. Otherwise, the family names up and down the block, which was half in Nutley and half in Belleville, were virtually all Italian: Lardier, Dimichino, Gingerelli, Troino, Francisco, Bonano, Buccino, Cerami, D'Ambola, all the way to the dead end.

More than a century ago, Italians came to our towns, following the 400-year-old example of Christopher Columbus, in search of a better life. Our Italian ancestors left the old country with little more than a suitcase or what they could carry away from a land that failed to feed them. In America, they found they could work and raise a family. And, with hard work, each generation would prosper from the Italians to the Italian Americans to the American Italians.

In the Italian neighborhoods, from Silver Lake in southern Belleville to Avondale in northeastern Nutley, and the enclaves in between, street life was the same as fruit vendors called out to the houses from horse-drawn carts. The *biancalina* man sold the bleach to make the linens white. Salesmen knocked on doors to sell insurance, Fuller brushes, or offered to sharpen knives.

The trades brought most of the Italian immigrants to Belleville and Nutley. The Italians worked hard, in the pre-Velodrome quarries of Nutley, in the factory sweatshops in Belleville. They broke their backs digging trenches for the towns' water mains and sewer systems. They built and worked the Morris Canal along the western border of our towns.

In the early days of the last century, when the largest influx of Italians immigrated to Belleville and Nutley, the border was an imaginary government line, as most Italian families in one town had relatives in the other town.

The towns were similarly dotted with old-family mansions and crowded apartments. In the Italian neighborhoods, among the extended families living within a few houses of each other, there were always gardens, fig trees, tomato plants, melons and other favorite greens. Small farms, such as my grandfather's, provided food, goat's milk, chickens, eggs and families drew water from hand-dug wells on many of these streets. Grapevines were familiar in town, and *compare* gathered each fall to make the wine of their forefathers.

Italians crisscrossed town borders, attending celebrations and patron saint feasts held at St. Peter's Church and St. Anthony's Church in Belleville, and religious celebrations, communions, confirmations and weddings at Holy Family and St. Mary's Church.

The towns had social clubs where men from the same villages and dialects gathered to talk about the old country and politics, while sipping espresso and smoking stogies. Many of our *mitigan* friends learned the slang of our fathers as we did and also appreciated our cooking. Pulitzer Prize winner Russell Baker wrote about his time growing up in Belleville and his esteemed favor of his friends' Italian foods.

We Italian Americans of Nutley and Belleville are proud of our ancestors and their sacrifice to make a better life for us. We continue many traditions from the old country, especially with meals at holidays. And we continue to work towards the goal of a better life that our forefathers gave up so much to make real for us.

We continue to educate ourselves and the next generations through chapter meetings of Unico National, the Italian-American service organization, featuring insights on our rich history, culture and heritage.

Thankful for growing up in old Belleville

I'm thankful for growing up in old Belleville. New Jersey, that is, not Belleville, Ontario, or Belleville, Illinois, or Belleville, Michigan, or Belleville, Kansas or even Belleville, Paris. I'm thankful for growing up in good old Belleville, New Jersey.

I'm thankful that I spent the first ten years of my life growing up in the same house my father grew up in and that his father built nearly a hundred years ago in Belleville, New Jersey.

I'm thankful for the second-floor four-room cold-water flat we shared those first ten years on Gless Avenue.

I'm thankful that my father's mother lived downstairs from us for a while, even though she spoke words I never understood and usually scared the daylights out of me.

I'm thankful for grandma's cats that wandered aimlessly and lived mostly in an abandoned car in the yard – just like in the famous play. And for her chickens, which somehow got along just fine with the cats.

I'm thankful grandma owned our house and the house next door and the land where her grapevines and gardens grew like a rich forest all the way up the hill to Newark Place.

I'm thankful for grandma's scary basement and the coal furnaces and the days when thunder roared inside our house as the coal man filled the bin through a side cellar window.

I'm thankful I played in that cellar long enough to sniff at the wine barrels and remember the wine press from grandma's second husband.

I'm thankful for snowstorms when I was a kid and got to play in them until my clothes were soaked through and I was shivering and thankful for Mom and warm, dry clothes. And for the pots of water she heated on the stove so I could take a hot bath.

I'm thankful for the ashes from the coal furnace that my dad shoveled on the ice under neighbors' car wheels spinning on the icy street.

I'm thankful for friends on Gless Avenue, Jerry the Ice Cream Man and the Mosquito Man and all those games we played in the dead end street.

I'm thankful for fields and woods to explore at the end of Gless Avenue and beyond the knoll near Smallwood Avenue.

We explored fields below power lines.

I'm thankful for friends from two old Belleville neighborhoods.

I'm thankful for our house on Carpenter Street and the long side lot where my friends and I played. And for the wide open fields behind the isolation hospital.

I'm thankful for my new best friend on Carpenter Street whose cousin I've been married to for more than thirty years.

I'm thankful for safe streets we walked and rode our bikes on in old Belleville.

I'm thankful for sledding at Forest Hills, and for learning how to ice skate in figure skates at the frozen basketball court at the end of Fairway Avenue, so we could all play hockey and once a year rent out the Branch Brook ice rink for a couple of hours.

I'm thankful for Belleville school teachers who were fair to me and gave me every opportunity to excel.

I'm thankful for our first apartment on Mary Street, and the winter storms that year and the parking spot fights that pushed us to find a house and a town that required driveways and off-street parking.

I'm thankful for the history of old Belleville which continues to reveal itself as we peel away layer upon layer and discover more rich and curious history in this little town.

I'm thankful for famous people who have lived here, whether or not they remember any of it, Russell Baker, Stephen Crane, Frances Goodrich, Nicky Arnold, Gene Hutmaker, and singers Connie Francis, Tommy DeVito and Frankie Valli.

And for those, like George Washington who may have passed through on their way somewhere else.

I'm thankful for our veterans who paved the way for all the things for which I am thankful.

I'm thankful for my cousin Raymond DeLuca who was killed in Vietnam while trying to aid a wounded comrade. And for the 160 brave young men from old Belleville who laid down their lives that I could grow up in a land of the free.

For my never-ending connections to growing up in old Belleville, I shall always be thankful.

About Anthony Buccino

Anthony Buccino writes with clarity and humor in his verse and in columns about growing up in the second half of the 20th century. He has been called "New Jersey's Garrison Keillor or something to that effect." Born in Belleville, the Nutley, N.J., resident published nineteen books. His writing about life in northern New Jersey has been published on Belleville Patch and NJ Voices. His transit writing on NJ.com earned a SPJ-NJ 2010 Excellence in Journalism award. He won two more EIJ awards in 2013.

Buccino was managing editor at Worrall Community Newspapers where he oversaw the Nutley Journal, The Belleville Post, The Independent Press of Bloomfield and The Glen Ridge Paper. Earlier he was editor of The Belleville Times. He has been published in The Wall Street Journal, New Jersey Monthly, the Passaic Herald News, New Jersey Federated Sportsmen, Italian Tribune, Behind the Lines and many literary publications.

A member of the Society of Professional Journalists, New Jersey Chapter, Buccino attended Montclair State College.

The poetry editors for U.S. 1 Worksheets nominated Buccino's poem "At The Vet" for the national Pushcart Prize. His poem "Jersey Geese" earned Honorable Mention in the 2011 Allen Ginsberg Poetry Awards. His poem "Something Tells Me You Went To Catholic School" earned Honorable Mention in the 2010 Allen Ginsberg Poetry Awards. His poem "Ten Minutes" earned Honorable Mention in the 2009 Allen Ginsberg Poetry Awards. "Hands In Socks" was named Editor's Choice in the 2008 Allen Ginsberg Poetry Awards.

Visit AnthonyBuccino.com

NUTLEY NOTABLES The men and women who made a memorable impact on our home town, Nutley, New Jersey

A FATHER'S PLACE - An Eclectic Collection

MARTHA STEWART DOESN'T LIVE HERE ANYMORE AND OTHER ESSAYS

RAMBLING ROUND, Inside and Outside at the Same Time

SISTER DRESSED ME FUNNY

THIS SEAT TAKEN? Notes of a Hapless Commuter

BELLEVILLE AND NUTLEY IN THE CIVIL WAR – A brief history

BELLEVILLE SONS HONOR ROLL

NUTLEY SONS HONOR ROLL

JERSEY CITY SNAPSHOTS

AMERICAN BOY: Pushing Sixty

CANNED - Booted, bumped, down-sized, fired, forced out, hated, hired, jobless, laid off, let go, out of work, out-sourced, pink-slipped, terminated, sacked, unemployed

ONE MORNING IN JERSEY CITY

RETRIEVING LABRADOR DAYS dog tales in prose and verse

SIXTEEN INCHES ON CENTER

SOMETIMES I SWEAR IN ITALIAN

VOICES ON THE BUS train, subway, sidewalk and in my head

YOUNTAKAH COUNTRY A Poetic View of Nutley, Old and New

All titles published by Cherry Blossom Press, available on Amazon